Methuen Drama

Published by Methuen Drama 2012

Methuen Drama, an imprint of Bloomsbury Publishing Plc

1 3 5 7 9 10 8 6 4 2

Methuen Drama
Bloomsbury Publishing Plc
50 Bedford Square
London WC1B 3DP
www.methuendrama.com

First published by Methuen Drama in 2012

ISBN 978 1 408 17247 6

A CIP catalogue record for this book is available from the British Library

Available in the USA from Bloomsbury Academic & Professional, 175 Fifth
Avenue/3rd Floor, New York, NY 10010. www.BloomsburyAcademicUSA.com

Typeset by Mark Heslington Ltd, Scarborough, North Yorkshire
Printed and bound in Great Britain by CPI Group (UK) Ltd, Croydon CR0 4YY

Live Theatre

presents the world premiere of

Nativities

By Zoe Cooper

Tuesday 14 February to Saturday 3 March 2012

The play was commissioned and first performed at
Live Theatre, Newcastle upon Tyne

A word from the writer

My first job after university was as a temp in a big internet company in a huge glass and metal business park. There were dress-down Fridays and donuts on Wednesdays and a lot of gossip. I was one of a big team of 'roaming' secretaries and people got my name wrong all the time. The work was repetitive, menial and sometimes just a bit degrading. Having said that, I also loved it – the easy banter, the routine of the work, and the fact that I absolutely understood my function in the job. It was a great contrast from the self-involved turmoil that I felt about relationships, my career beyond that role and my place in the world. I have wanted to write about someone setting out in life like that ever since, and about what a place of work can mean to lots of people at lots of different ages. This is that play.

Nativities

BY **Zoe Cooper**

Cast

Paul Woodson David
Sam Neale Stella
Christopher Connel Clive
Phillippa Wilson Louise
Melanie Hill Madge
Laura Norton Chelle

Creative & Production Team

Zoe Cooper Writer
Max Roberts Director
Gary McCann Designer
Drummond Orr Lighting Designer & Production Manager
Dave Flynn Sound Designer
Paul Aziz AV Designer & Stage Manager
Heather Robertson Deputy Stage Manager
Lou Duffy Costume Supervisor
Mark Tolan Senior Technician
Tom Saunders Technician
Rosie Kellagher Assistant Director
Gez Casey Script Advisor/Dramaturg
Lucy Jenkins CDG Casting
Sooki McShane CDG Casting

Paul Callaghan Chair
Jim Beirne Chief Executive
Max Roberts Artistic Director
Wendy Barnfather Operations Director

Cast

Paul Woodson David

Theatre credits include: *Young Pretender* (Edinburgh and tour), *The Merry Wives of Windsor* (Globe Theatre and tour), *Three Sisters* (Lyric Hammersmith), *As You Like It* (Palace Theatre, Watford), *Romeo & Juliet* (Globe Theatre) and *We That are Left* (Palace Theatre, Watford).

Television and film credits include: *Eternal Law* (Kudos) and *Day of the Triffids* (BBC).

Samantha Neale Stella

Theatre credits include: *The Girls From Poppyfield Close* and *Big Society* (Live Theatre) and *Dick Whittington* (Gibber Theatre Company).

Television and film credits include: *Eternal Law* and *Vera* (ITV), *Frank* (I Like Films Me Ltd), *Married, Single, Other* (Left Bank Pictures), *The Alexander Wilson Project* (A.W. Internet project), *No Place* (24/25 Films), *Other Child* (Team Worxx) and *Interview With a Hitman* (Scanner/Rhodes).

Christopher Connel Clive

Theatre credits include: *The Pitman Painters* (Live Theatre/National Theatre/Samuel J. Friedman Theatre on Broadway), *Cooking with Elvis* and *Toast* (Live Theatre), *Shooting the Legend* (Theatre Royal Newcastle), *Cooking With Elvis*, *Studs*, *Up on Roof* and *A Kick in the Baubles* (Hull Truck), *Bouncers* (Hull Truck Number 1 Tour), *Black on White Shorts* (Paines

Plough/Live Theatre), *And a Nightingale Sang* (Cheltenham Everyman), *The Steal* and *Men Women Inspectors and Dogs* (Theatre Royal York/Cloud Nine), *Peer Gynt* (Three Over Eden Theatre Company), *The Fillacavity Hote* (Kinetic Theatre Company), *Cuddys Miles* (Customs House), *Unreal* (Cloud Nine), *Peer Gynt* (Three Over Eden), *The Purple Pullover* (Cloud Nine) and productions with Bruvvers Theatre Company.

Television and film credits include: the feature films *Goal* (Milkshake Films/Touchstone Pictures) and *Purely Belter* (FilmFour/Mumbo Jumbo Productions), *Emmerdale, Heatbeat* and *How We Used to Live* (YTV), *The Round Tower* (Festival Films), *Badger* (BBC/Feelgood Fiction), *The Bill* (ITV), *Byker Grove* (BBC/Zenith), *Quayside* (Zenith/Tyne Tees), *King Leek* (Granada Television), *Crocodile Shoes*, *George Gently* and the sitcom *Breeze Block* (BBC), *The Block* (Channel 4), *Take Me* (Scottish TV/Coastal Productions), *Steel River Blues* (Granada), *Lawless* (Company/ITV) and *Navy of the Damned* (PDTV).

Phillippa Wilson Louise

Theatre credits include: *The Pitmen Painters* (Live Theatre/National Theatre/Samuel J. Friedman Theatre on Broadway), *A Walk On Part*, *The Girls From Poppyfield Close*, *Twelve Tales of Tyneside*, *Here I Come*, *Some Like it Cold*, *The Beautiful Game*, *Oh What a Lovely War*, *Bandits*, *For The Crack* and *1990* (Live Theatre), *Writing Wrongs* and *Waiting for Gateaux* (Customs House), *Stars In The Morning Sky*, *The Long Line*, *Beauty and the Beast*, *Cinderella*, *The Snow Queen* and *Merlin the Magnificent* (Northern Stage), *The Importance of Being Earnest*, *A Nightingale Sang* and *The Real Inspector Hound* (Queen's Hall, Hexham), *Billy Liar* and *Hay Fever* (Astrakhan Theatre Company), *The Grand Finale*, *Hatched and Dispatched* and *Back by Christmas* (Living Memory Theatre Company).

Television and film credits include: *Empathy* (Carnival Films), *Tracy Beaker Returns*, *The Student Prince*, *EastEnders* and *Casualty* (BBC), *Clay*, *Holby City*, *Doctors* and *Byker Grove* (BBC/Zenith), *Where the Heart Is* (United Television), *Badger* (BBC/Feelgood Fiction), *The Royal* and *Heartbeat* (Yorkshire Television), *55 Degrees North*, *Firm Friends* and *Spender* (Zenith Productions), *Rebus* (ITV/Clerkenwell Films), *Emmerdale* (Granada Television), *The Bill* (Thames Television), *Dead Terry* and *Sub Zero* (Superkrush and Subzero Productions).

Melanie Hill Madge

Theatre credits include: *Inheritance* (Live Theatre), *Maggie's End* (Shaw Theatre), *Tongue of a Bird* (Almeida Theatre), *Cardiff East* (Royal National), *I Have Been Here Before* (Royal Exchange), *Women Beware Women* (Royal Court) and *Educating Rita* (British American Theatre Institute).

Television and film credits include: *Waterloo Road*, *United*, *Merlin*, *Body Farm* and *Bread* (BBC), *Candy Cabs* (Splash Media), *Joe Maddison's War* (Mammoth Screen), *The Thick Of It*, *Holby City* and *Rather You Than Me* (BBC), *White Girl* (Tiger Aspect), *The Street II* (ITV Productions), *Cape Wrath* (Ecosse TV Productions), *Emmerdale* and *Hot Money* (Granada), *Playing The Field* (Tiger Aspect), *Crocodile Shoes* (Red Rooster/BBC), *Finney* (Zenith), *Auf Wiedersehen Pet* (Central), *Unconditional* (Stone City Films), *Stardust* (Paramount), *Brassed Off* (Prominent Features/ Channel 4), *When Saturday Comes* (Capitol Films) and *28k* (filmflow production).

Laura Norton Chelle

Theatre credits include: *Faith & Cold Reading*, *You Couldn't Make it Up*, *You Really Couldn't Make it Up*, *Jump!*, *A Nightingale Sang* and *Smack Family Robinson* (Live Theatre), *Keepers of the Flame* (Live Theatre/Royal Shakespeare Company), *Jack and the Beanstalk*, *Writing Wrong* and *Lucky Numbers* (Customs House), *The Weather Kitchen* (Monster Productions), *Immaculate Deception* (New Writing North), *Tonic* and *A Twist of Lemon* (Open Clasp Theatre Company) and *Hansel and Gretel* (Northern Stage).

Television and film credits include: *Vera*, *The Royal Today* and *Steel River Blues* (ITV), *Angel Cake* and *Badger* (BBC), *55 Degrees North* (Zenith Productions), *Byker Grove* (BBC/Zenith), *Would Like to Meet* (Pinball Films), *Aggro* (Shakabuku Films), *Apple Crush* (Dene Films), *The Royal Today* (YTV drama) and a drama documentary about *Nelson* (Seneca Productions for Channel 4).

Creative & Production Team

Zoe Cooper Writer

Zoe is a playwright and theatre practitioner who first came to Live
Theatre's attention during *Different Stages*, the company's 2010
New Writing Festival. After graduating with an MPhil in Playwriting
from the University of Birmingham in 2010 she went on to write
short plays for Nabokov, Theatre503 and the Tristan Bates Theatre.
Zoe has also been working with the National Theatre Studio
developing a project based on the Strindberg play *The Father*
and with the RSC studio on a new play.

Nativities is Zoe's first full length play commission.

Max Roberts Director

Max Roberts is Artistic Director and founding member of Live
Theatre, Newcastle upon Tyne. Productions directed for the
company include *The Long Line*, *Yesterday's Children*, *Long
Shadows*, *The Filleting Machine* and *Seafarers* by Tom Hadaway, *A
Nightingale Sang*, *Operation Elvis* and *Bandits* by C. P. Taylor, *Close
the Coalhouse Door*, *Going Home*, *Shooting the Legend*, *Tales from
the Backyard* and *Charlie's Trousers* by Alan Plater, *In Blackberry
Time* by Alan Plater and Michael Chaplin from the stories of Sid
Chaplin, *Come Snow Come Blow* by Leonard Barras, *Northern
Glory* and *Kidder's Luck* by Phil Woods, *The Ghost of Dan Smith*
and *The Great Fire of Newcastle* by Peter Flannery, *The Women
Who Painted Ships* by Julia Darling, *A Northern Odyssey* by
Shelagh Stephenson, *Bones* and *Noir* by Peter Straughan, *Lush
Life* by Paul Sirett, *You Couldn't Make It Up* and *You Really Couldn't
Make It Up* by Michael and Tom Chaplin, *Cooking with Elvis*, *NE1*,
Wittgenstein on Tyne and *The Pitmen Painters* by Lee Hall (which
was commissioned to open the newly refurbished Live Theatre in
September 2007). After celebrated seasons at Live Theatre, the
National Theatre and on Broadway as well as two UK tours *The
Pitmen Painters* opened in the West End at the Duchess Theatre in
October 2011 produced in association with Live Theatre, National
Theatre and Bill Kenwright Ltd. Max has also recently directed *A
Walk On Part*, adapted by Michael Chaplin from the diaries of Chris

Mullin (*Decline & Fall* and *A View From The Foothills*). The play has gone on to enjoy successful runs at Soho Theatre, London and is to be revived in March 2012.

Gary McCann Designer

Gary McCann is originally from County Armagh, Northern Ireland, and trained at Nottingham Trent University. He has worked extensively in his native Ireland and across the UK, as well as internationally, in the fields of theatre, opera, TV, interior and event design.

Recent and forthcoming design work includes: *A Walk On Part* (Live Theatre/Soho Theatre), *The Pitmen Painters* (Live Theatre/National Theatre/Samuel J. Friedman Theatre on Broadway/West End), *33 Variations* and *In Zeichen Der Kunst* (Volkstheater, Vienna), *Die Fledermaus* (National Opera of Norway), *La Voix Humaine* and *L'Heure Espagnole* (National Touring Opera of Holland), *Three Days in May* (National Tour, West End), *The Girl in the Yellow Dress* (Market Theatre, Johannesburg/Grahamstown Festival/Live Theatre/Stadtheater Stockholm), *Someone Who'll Watch Over Me* and *Moonlight and Magnolias* (Perth Theatre), *Cosi Fan Tutte* (Schonnbrunn Palace, Vienna) *Norma* (National Opera of Moldova), *Fidelio* (Garsington Opera), *Grimm Tales* (Library Theatre, Manchester), *Guys and Dolls* (Theater Bielefeld, Germany), *Owen Wingrave*, *La Pietra del Paragone* (Opera Trionfo, Amsterdam), *A Northern Odyssey*, *Me & Cilla*, *Top Girls* and *Motherland* (Live Theatre), *Cosi Fan Tutte* (Royal Academy of Music), *There's Something About Simmy* (Theatre Royal Stratford East and tour), *Home by Now* (BALTIC), *Thieves' Carnival*, *Broken Glass* (Watermill Theatre, Newbury), *Hurricane* (Arts Theatre London/59th St Theatre New York), *Protestants* (Soho Theatre), *The Little Prince*, *Much Ado About Nothing*, *The Glass Menagerie*, *The Man of Mode*, *Twelfth Night* and *Iphigeneia* (Lyric Theatre, Belfast), and *Song of the Western Men* (Chichester Festival Theatre). His work has been exhibited at the V&A museum in two exhibitions: *Collaborators* and *Transformation/Revelation*.

About Live Theatre

From its base on Newcastle's quayside, Live Theatre produces work as varied and diverse as the audiences it engages with. To do this it:

- Creates and performs new plays of world class quality

- Finds and develops creative talent

- Unlocks the potential of young people through theatre.

Founded in 1973, the theatre was recently transformed via a £5.5 million redevelopment. The result is a beautifully restored and refurbished complex of five Grade II listed buildings with state-of-the-art facilities in a unique historical setting, including a 160-seat cabaret style theatre, a studio theatre, renovated rehearsal rooms, a series of dedicated writer's rooms as well as a thriving café, bar and pub.

www.live.org.uk

 Supported by **ARTS COUNCIL ENGLAND**

 **Newcastle** City Council

Nativities

For Mum

Characters

David, *thirty-seven, Call Centre Manager*
Madge, *fifty-three, Team Leader and Call Centre Advisor*
Chelle, *twenty-four, team member and Call Centre Advisor*
Clive, *thirty-four, team member and Call Centre Advisor*
Louise, *thirty-seven, ultrasound nurse*
Stella, *eighteen, Team Admin Assistant*

Author's notes:

[/] Indicates the point at which the speaker is cut across

Speech in square brackets – '[example]' – indicates words implied or what would have been said if the speaker had not been cut off

The author would like to say thank you to Max, Gez and Rosie for their faith, support and intelligent work; all the people I have lived with at 280a, especially Jane for being the first person to make me feel I should have a go at this, and Tom for all the tea breaks when I discussed at length why I couldn't; my agent Lily; my dad and Kate; and finally to my sister Emily for her hilarious and intelligent insights into the world of the call centre.

One

A large open-plan office with a kitchen area. **Stella** *is standing awkwardly in the middle of the office. She is wearing cheap office clothes.* **David** *is standing some way from her. He's just arrived and is still wearing his coat. He is out of breath.* **David** *takes his coat off through the following.*

David   I had to run up the /

Stella   I didn't /

David   Because the lift is broken so I had to /

Stella   I didn't see anyone /

David   I had to run up all those stairs to be here on time and now he is not here.

Stella   Because I was actually here at eight and I didn't see anyone come in.

Beat.

David   My forehead's wet with it . . .

Stella   You are the first person I've seen /

David (*wiping his forehead*)   That is disgusting.

Beat.

Stella   I had to wear two jumpers this morning /

David   I hate it when I drip like that /

Stella   Two jumpers and a scarf under my coat /

David   When I sweat so heavily /

Stella   I had to really wrap up /

David   When I *perspire* so profusely /

Stella   But it's very /

David   And just after I've put on a new shirt /

Stella   But it's very warm in here isn't it? /

David   Because I am really just sweating straight . . . straight through the material.

Beat.

. . . what?

Beat.

Sorry, what did you . . .?

Stella   Because I was dead cold as I walked here this morning but now it feels really hot in here /

David   That's what I'm saying /

Stella   Sorry /

David   That is what I am saying, that is why I'm /

Stella   Sorry /

David   The heating is stuck on high and I'm here to show the engineers what the problem is.

Stella   I'm sorry, I talk too much when I'm nervous. When I'm feeling a bit . . . nervous.

Beat.

David (*moving slightly*)   Christ, I feel a bit. A bit strange.

Stella   Would you like a glass of water?

David   Those stairs!

Stella   Shall I get you a glass of water?

David   Those bloody stairs.

Beat.

Oh. Yes. Yes.

Stella *goes to the tap and runs* **David** *a glass of water.*

David *smiles at* **Stella**.

Stella *smiles back at* **David**.

Stella *hands* **David** *the water*.

David *drinks quite a bit of the water,* **Stella** *watches him.*

David   Of course this isn't really my job.

Stella   No /

David   It is not as if this is actually in my job description /

Stella   It's really good of you to get here early just to let them in /

David   Sweat drip drip dripping on to my eyebrows /

Stella   Because it's hardly your job is it?

David   Sweat dripping down me and my heart banging in my chest after that run up those stairs and this isn't even what I am paid to do, not what I am being paid for at all.

Beat.

Stella   Maybe you should sit down /

David   I think I'm going to have to have a little sit down actually /

Stella   Take the weight off your feet and just sit /

David   I am very busy today and so I don't really have time for this but I am that puffed out, that physically puffed out from running up those stairs I am going to have to have a little sit. Sit down here for a minute and get my breath back.

David *sits down heavily.*

That's better. I feel better for that now. For having sat down. Feel much better for having done that.

Beat.

Because the engineer, the heating engineer was meant to sort it out last week but then he said that actually with this sort of . . . because apparently it's broken in two places. It's the generator but it's also the fan, which strikes me as strange, strikes me as a bit odd, because it's not the air con that we're, that is not the bit that's /

Stella   But it's all connected isn't it /

David   What?

Stella   Air con and the, the heating . . . it's one system to regulate the whole /

David   Yes I know /

Stella   To regulate the atmosphere in the office /

David   I know /

Stella   The air quality in the office /

David   I *understand*.

Stella   Sorry /

David   I mean Christ, it's my bloody office, of course I *understand* /

Stella   Sorry /

David   I mean Christ, I am the bloody manager of this thing aren't I?

Stella   Sorry, yes . . .

Beat.

David (*jovially*)   I run this bloody place, I should bloody understand shouldn't I? Excuse my French but I should fucking understand shouldn't I?

Beat.

In the end he decided it was a two-man job and anyway he needed a spare part which of course he didn't have so he had to go away and come back this morning with this extra man and this extra part and no doubt, no doubt and probably a third man and all of them all standing around debating the various merits of the air con, the heating and the air con and God knows what else like old, like a bunch of old *women* this morning. So I was fully expecting that. I was expecting them to be here this morning and tell me that.

Beat.

I was . . . I was resigned I suppose. That was OK, but then I arrive and there is no one /

Stella No one's here /

David There is no one actually here apart from you /

Stella You are the only one here.

David And I mean if we don't, if I don't get it fixed people, you know, people working here, because I do try to be patient, I try to be reasonable because I am after all, I am a reasonable boss and I do try to treat everyone as a colleague rather than, well rather than a subordinate I suppose but you do get to the point . . . because it is any excuse, it is really any excuse with some people not to work, not to come in to work, like really it is unreasonable for them to work in any sort of *heat* /

Stella And with the noise too /

David Like they can't /

Stella Chalk on blackboard /

David Like they cannot possibly tolerate /

Stella Like teeth on cotton /

David Tolerate any sort of 'unpleasantness' /

Stella A grating sort of noise. Because it's been broken for a while hasn't it? Madge says it goes straight through her. That noise. The noise of the fan. The fan in the air con. (*Putting her hand on her chest.*) Goes straight through her.

Pause.

David   Sorry. I.

Stella   Yes?

David   I don't think we have . . .

Stella   Yes?

David   It's just that I thought that I . . . well I assumed . . .

Stella   Yes?

David   I assumed you were here with the cleaners.

Stella   No.

David   Oh.

Stella   No.

Beat.

No. Because we have actually met / [before]

David (**David** *looks at* **Stella** *more closely.*) Have we?

Stella   Yes /

David   *Have* we /

Stella   It's /

David   *Have* we /

Stella   It's OK.

Beat.

David   Because I don't, if I'm honest I don't /

Stella   It's a big office /

David   Because it is and sometimes /

Stella   And it must be difficult with all those names to remember.

Beat.

David   Because I do know your face.

Stella   Do you?

David   Recognise your /

Stella   Maybe I have that sort of face /

David   Like I have seen you /

Stella   Familiar. Like you might /

David   Seen you before somewhere /

Stella   Sort of face you think you have seen around before /

David   But then I thought with you being here so early that you were with the / cleaners

Stella   But you haven't actually, you haven't actually seen it before, it is just sort of a generic sort of face.

Beat.

David (*laughing*)   I see. That's very funny. That is really very funny. You are very funny.

Stella   I'm Stella.

David   Stella?

Stella   Like a star.

Beat.

You interviewed me for my job last month. I started last week. Last Monday.

Beat.

David   I am /

Stella   Are you /

David   Think I am remembering /

Stella   Are you /

David   Because I thought, I did think . . .

Stella   Because you appointed me as the administrative
assistant for Madge's team and I have been . . .

David   I did think . . . I would have remembered a face as
pretty as that.

Pause.

Stella   You were wearing a yellow tie /

David   I just couldn't quite place /

Stella   Mustard tie /

David   Couldn't quite place you /

Stella   Blue suit /

David   Not straight off /

Stella   And white shirt. In the interview. You said. You told
me. That your girlfriend dresses you.

Beat.

David   Ha! /

Stella   I think it's lovely /

David   Ha! Don't remember at /

Stella   I think it's lovely of her /

David   I don't remember that at / all

Stella   Really lovely /

David   I'm probably old enough to pick out my own tie
but she enjoys it and anyway she has me wrapped. She has
me wrapped round her little finger and pressed up under
her thumb.

Stella   So /

David   She has me in the palm of her hand. Has me sat in
the very palm of her hand /

Stella   So romantic /

David Me sat in her palm /

Stella So romantic of her, of both of you really. For Kirsten to dress you like that.

Beat.

David Sorry, how did you . . .

Stella You mentioned her in the interview.

David Right.

Stella You said you've just started in the job yourself.

David Right.

Stella You joked that we could both be new kids together. Because you only joined a few months ago yourself you said. You had only started in the job a few months before that so we would be like new children together on the first day at school.

Beat.

I thought I'd probably got it when you said that /

David That was naughty of me /

Stella I wanted to say actually Mr Thwaite /

David Very naughty indeed /

Stella I wanted to say /

David I must have /

Stella Because I never got to /

David I must have been distracted /

Stella I haven't had the chance to say /

David Probably got distracted. (*Smiling.*) You probably distracted me.

Beat.

Because I probably shouldn't have said that /

Stella   I haven't had the chance to say how *grateful* /

David   Not in line with best / practice

Stella   How *grateful* I am that you gave me this opportunity /

David   Not in line with best practice at all because I probably should not have indicated to you like. I probably should not have let on like that that you had probably already got the job /

Stella   Because the opportunity to work here is just so / [important to me]

David   You probably should not, you probably should not tell people that I said that. That I said that about being new kids together, like you had already got the job.

Beat.

Because we don't want people thinking that I was biased do we Stephanie /

Stella   It's /

David   I said we don't want anyone thinking I gave you the job /

Stella   It's /

David   That I gave you the job because of anything other than your performance in that interview.

Stella   It's not Stepha[nie actually.]

David   We don't want that do we?

Pause.

Stella   It's my first job you see /

David   Yes /

Stella   My first job and I really /

David Yes /

Stella It really feels like I've landed on my feet. Everyone is so nice. So I wanted to say how grateful. How grateful I am that you have given me this chance.

Two

The sounds of a garden in winter: the wind and a nearby road.
Louise *is standing in her and* **Clive**'s *kitchen. She is looking out at the garden through cheap French windows.* **Clive** *is sitting at the table behind her. They both have tea.*

Clive I just. I like that pond.

Beat.

I like the frogs.

Louise You never even /

Clive I like watching them in the spring, tadpoles and /

Louise You hardly /

Clive Circle of life and that.

Louise You've hardly been out there in months though have you though, either of us, neither of us have been out there for months and months.

Clive It's winter /

Louise Yes, but /

Clive It's midwinter. Of course I've not been out there for a while. It's the middle of winter.

Beat.

Louise We can't just sit on our hands /

Clive It's not like there is any great / *hurry.*

Louise I don't want us to just sit on our hands and wait /

Clive   Ages before we / need to start

Louise   Because he could be crawling /

Clive   Before we need to start thinking about /

Louise   Crawling and fall in. He could fall in your pond.

Beat.

The doctor said /

Clive   I know /

Louise   He said we could start planning /

Clive   I know.

Louise   That we should.

Clive   I know. I do know what he said.

Beat.

Louise   Goodness knows I'm not finding it /

Clive   That's not /

Louise   Going through it all again.

Beat.

I don't find this any easier than you do Clive.

Beat.

Clive   I just like the pond /

Louise   But we do have to start thinking about it /

Clive   I just like that pond Louise. I like having that pond in my garden. I don't want to dig it up. That's all. I don't want to dig my pond up.

Pause.

Louise (*smiling*)   Actually we would fill it in.

Clive   What?

Louise We would fill it in not / dig it

Clive Right /

Louise Because that's the nature of a hole isn't it. You have to fill it in for it not to be /

Clive Alright /

Louise For it to not be there any more.

Clive Alright Louise.

Pause.

Louise Have you spoken to work?

Beat.

You will need to.

Beat.

To get cover.

Beat.

They might have to train someone /

Clive Didn't train me when I /

Louise Because Claire, Claire, our senior staff nurse Claire, when she had her little girl /

Clive Didn't train me when / I

Louise There was quite a lot of planning /

Clive Because actually they could get a trained monkey to /

Louise Me and the rest of the ward had to spend quite a lot of time talking it /

Clive I suppose they will need time to train the monkey /

Louise We spent ages trying to juggle the schedules and in the end we had to get a /

Clive   To train the monkey to answer the phone in the correct company manner.

Louise   We had to get a locum in to cover the /

Clive   'Hello, you are through to Scion Communications. How can I help you? I will register that complaint now, I will send you through the forms for that complaint, I will pass on the information about that complaint. I will register that complaint and pass your concerns on /'

Louise   Clive.

Clive   'I understand that / you are'

Louise   Clive.

Clive   'I understand that you are angry.'

Beat.

Louise   You're the one that wanted to take the time off.

Clive   'I understand you are angry. I understand that you are *angry*. But there is really, there is nothing I can, I personally, nothing I can do. All I can do is pass on the complaint sir. That is all I as a monkey, as a trained primate am able to do.'

Louise   You said that you wanted to take the paternity . . . the paternity leave if you could. That's all. That's all I'm saying. That's all that I was saying. I was just reminding you what you said you wanted. You said you wanted to be at home.

Beat.

Clive   I'll talk to them tomorrow.

Beat.

Louise   We could always cover it over I suppose.

Clive   What?

Louise   The pond.

Clive   Oh.

Louise   With a hard cover or something.

Beat.

Clive   When I was little we had a pond. Me and my sister would watch for the tadpoles.

Louise   We can always dig it out again.

Clive   Like tapioca.

Louise   When he gets big enough.

Clive   Yes.

Louise   Big enough to appreciate it properly.

Clive and **Louise** *look at each other.* **Louise** *is sort of smiling,* **Clive** *looks back out over the garden. The sound of winter swells.*

Three

The whir of the office air conditioning fan as it tries to start up; it does so two or three times. The noise is crunching, loud and mechanical. It cuts out. The end of the day at the office. **David** *is putting his coat on, he has his back slightly to* **Madge**. **Madge** *stands a small distance from him, holding her handbag and coat.* **Stella** *is sitting behind a desk sorting some papers methodically.*

Madge   For a traditional Sunday lunch,

David   Her mum cooked,

Madge   And I bet she makes a lovely spread,

David   And the whole tribe was there, her two sisters and their children.

Madge (*fondly*)   All the little ones.

David   Her sisters and their husbands and their children.

Madge   And all the tiny children playing, running round the house, playing and causing havoc and getting under everyone's feet.

David   And after we have eaten he makes me stand out in the garden with him.

Madge   Oh?

David   Just me and him.

Madge   Oh yes?

David   And we smoke these cigars.

Madge   Goodness.

David   Like I was his son.

Madge   Well you are practically /

David   Felt like I was his son /

Madge   Are practically /

David   Like I was his family /

Madge   Are practically family.

David   His kith and kin.

Beat.

And he just said thankyou /

Madge   Thankyou?

David   'Thankyou for being such a' /

Madge   Oh David, I'm filling up / [here]

David   '. . . because my daughter is so special' /

Madge   You are making me fill up here /

David   'My daughter is so special to me so I want to say thankyou. I just wanted to say thankyou. Thankyou for

making her so happy.' And we just stood there, just stood
there puffing away together. Just the two of us. Puffing away.

Madge *beams.*

David   Like two peas /

Madge   And are you spending Christmas /

David   Like two identical peas in a pod /

Madge   Are you Christmasing with them then?

David   Just the two of us identical peas from the exact same
pod stood there by the rotating gazebo and the ride-on
mower and opposite the four Japanese cars in his – in
Michael's driveway, all the tiny children running around and
the general sense, the really general sense of bonhomie and
the two of us at the centre of all this stood there puffing. Just
puffing away together like we were born to it, like we were
born from the same pod.

Beat.

Madge   Christmas, are you /

David   Oh of course /

Madge   Of course you are. Of course you are spending the
whole of the Christmas season at Michael and Marie's.

Madge *beams.*

Because just imagine, Mr Wells's daughter, you marrying Mr
Wells's daughter. You marrying the heir. You the heir to all
this. Like in a fairytale. It's like you are in a fairytale isn't it?
You the commoner, just a common Jack working a job as the
Deputy Manager of this call centre and Kirsten, the princess,
the beautiful blonde princess in the castle on the hill and
your eyes met across a crowded room, a crowded call centre
floor I should say and now you are the heir of all that you
survey now in your kingdom, in Scion Communications, in
what will be your kingdom now.

Beat.

David   Well I should /

Madge   We're having a Christmas pudding to ourselves this year /

David   I should probably go /

Madge   I am quite looking forward to it actually because /

David   Because I did tell Kirsten that /

Madge   Because in the end you don't want to go running around /

David   Because I've been doing a lot of late nights and I did tell her that /

Madge   Running around rather than really, yes really enjoying the /

David   I did say I would be back before eight /

Madge   Because when I was younger and we would have my little Harry back from college or home for Christmas or even before that when he was still tiny and we would have all the cousins and the uncles and aunties and everyone all over for Christmas I would have to start planning the whole thing weeks, literally months in advance and by the time it got to Christmas it would just be, well, and I don't mind telling you, I would just be dead on my feet so it is really, it is really much better now (bless them but) much better now that it is just me and him indoors to worry about. Nothing to worry about but us, we just, we can just sit, we can sit all day watching the TV and eat. Just sit all day in our nightclothes stuffing our faces in front of the TV if that is what we want to do, which we don't of course, of course we don't actually *do* that but we could, that is the point, we could if we wanted to.

Beat.

David   Well I should probably be / [off]

Madge   Because when I was younger we used to do
Christmasses like that, like yours will be at Michael and
Marie's and don't get me wrong they were great, they were
fantastic, and I know that you and Kirsten and Michael
and Marie are going to be just fantastic, you are going to
be just fantastic.

Beat.

David (*indicating* **Madge**'s *coat*)   May I?

Madge   Such a gentleman.

David *helps* **Madge** *on with her coat.*

David *seems about to leave, he hovers near the door.*

Madge   I'll have to be careful though /

David   Right /

Madge   All that food /

David   Right /

Madge   All that rich food. Because I was thinking /

David   Right /

Madge   I don't want to go putting on /

David   Right /

Madge   I don't want to go getting fat do I?

David   Right. No.

Beat.

Madge   I don't want to be, back here in January, everyone
all . . . and me, the oldest /

David   No . . .

Madge   Me much older than the rest of you /

David   Surely / [not]

Madge   Already the oldest and now, now end up 'that fat wife, that fat wifey in the office' that everyone /

David   You could never be /

Madge   Aren't you a /

David   Not in the least bit /

Madge   Aren't you the charmer /

David   You're womanly /

Madge   No wonder the ladies /

David   All those lovely curves, how women are meant /

Madge   No wonder they all love you.

David   Do they?

Madge   Cheeky. They love you.

David   I had no /

Madge   Playing the innocent.

David   I had no idea.

Madge   Playing the innocent, pretending like you don't know how much all the ladies love you.

Beat.

My Malcolm barely notices me these days (bless him) but he barely notices I am there, I could be, I could be anyone.

David   That's /

Madge   Barely remembers I'm his wife I think.

David   Poor Madge /

Madge   I don't want you to go feeling sorry for /

David   Lovely lady like /

Madge   Don't you go feeling sorry for this stupid great lump. Don't you go feeling sorry for me David.

Beat.

She's very lucky.

David Sorry?

Madge Your Kirsten /

David Oh right /

Madge Very lucky woman. (*Patting **David**, motherly.*) Doesn't know how lucky she is.

David *goes to switch off the light and sees **Stella**, who is now sitting illuminated by her desk lamp.*

David Christ /

Madge (*surprised*) Are you still /

David Christ Stephanie /

Madge Gave us both quite a fright didn't she David /

David I didn't see you /

Stella Sorry /

David I didn't see you at all.

Madge Were you hiding /

Stella No /

Madge Hiding from us /

Stella No /

Madge Waiting to jump out /

Stella No /

Madge Hiding in the dark /

Stella No /

Madge Hiding in the dark and waiting to jump out and give us a fright?

Stella   No I /

Madge   To scare the living daylights out of us eh David? To make us jump out of our skins.

Beat.

Shift finished /

Stella   I know /

Madge   Finished twenty minutes ago.

Stella   I . . .

Beat.

Madge (*to* **David**)   She's that dedicated this one /

David   I know /

Madge   That dedicated we have to keep an eye on her /

David   Do we?

Madge   Else she might never /

David (*to* **Stella**)   Haven't you got a home to /

Madge   Might never go home.

Stella   I'm just finishing something off.

Beat.

Madge   Time you went. I don't want my right-hand woman, the linchpin in my team getting tired do I David? Especially in her . . . well I shouldn't say really should /

Stella   I'm / [fine]

Madge   Especially with David here.

Beat.

Doesn't she look nice though David?

David   Yes /

Madge Blooming.

Stella I'm sorry Madge /

Madge That is the word – 'blooming' . . .

Beat.

You probably want me to keep quiet. Probably thinking, 'Shut up Madge, why can't you just shut up.'

Stella (*appalled*) No /

Madge Just 'Shut up Madge.'

Beat.

I quite understand it. You don't want to jinx it. I was the same with my Harry. Look at him standing there. (*To* **David**.) You haven't got a clue what we are talking about have you?

David (*to* **Madge**) What?

Madge Not a clue, bless him. But we women just know don't we Stella? We have a sense for these things.

Madge *smiles at* **Stella** *maternally.*

You make me feel quite . . . you, sitting there in that state. And with this time of year as well. This season, Christmas just round the corner . . . because we were just talking, we were just talking about Christmas, about Christmas and family and what it all . . . what it all means weren't we David? Just talking about what it is all about and even though I am not, I'm not religious myself. That's not . . . it's not that I am religious all of a sudden but you make me think of . . . of myself I suppose. Of myself when I was much younger and Christmas was coming and I was in the state that you are in now. Makes me feel quite nostalgic. You make me feel quite nostalgic Stella.

Madge *wipes a tear from her eye.*

Listen to me . . . listen to me . . . I should . . . I should . . . it's time for me to go.

Madge *leaves*.

(*off*) Go home soon Stella.

David *looks at* **Stella**, *assessingly*.

David (*with a wink*)   Goodnight Stephanie.

We see **Stella** *for a moment, alone in the office in her pool of light.*

Four

Chelle *is lying on a hospital gurney with her top pulled up above her belly. She is heavily pregnant.* **Louise** *is setting up an ultrasound machine. She is also pregnant, but not as far along as* **Chelle** *and you would be forgiven for not noticing immediately.* **Chelle** *is playing with the hair at the back of her head. During the course of the scene she pulls strands out absently.*

Louise   Was it still snowing?

Chelle   Sorry?

Louise   When I left this morning it had just started to snow.

Chelle   Oh.

Louise   It doesn't normally settle does it?

Chelle   I suppose . . .

Louise   It normally disappears doesn't it, before you have a chance to really, to really look at it normally but I think it probably will, probably will settle this time.

Pause.

Chelle   It was howling.

Louise   Howling?

Chelle   The wind. Whipped round my face.

Louise   It's so beautiful /

Chelle The wind whipping round my face and me struggling, all duck-footed up that / [hill]

Louise So beautiful that you don't even notice the cold do you? /

Chelle All duck-footed. Feet like a duck. Like a duck up that hill. A cunting duck struggling up that cunting hill . . . duck-footed up that cunting hill. Must have looked a right cunt.

Beat.

Louise I didn't even notice how cold it was this morning it was that beautiful.

Chelle It goes right through me. That cold. I can feel it going right through me (*She puts her hand to her chest.*) right through me.

Louise It feels right, Christmas, the snow, the cold it feels /

Chelle I get that cold.

Louise It feels right. (*Holding a tube of ultrasound gel.*) I am going to put the /

Chelle Right.

Louise It will feel a bit /

Chelle OK.

Louise *starts to apply the gel to* **Chelle**'s *stomach.*

Chelle What are you calling yours?

Louise What /

Chelle What are you going to call yours?

Beat.

Louise James. He's called James.

Chelle Does he kick you?

Louise   What?

Chelle   James. Mine does.

Louise   He is just letting you know he is there.

Chelle   But do you ever feel. Do you ever feel that your baby /

Louise   Baby just likes to let you know that he is there.

Beat.

Chelle   Should I not have asked?

Louise   What?

Chelle   I just wanted to know if it was normal and I thought with you being /

Louise   No, it's OK. (*Placing a hand protectively on her belly.*) I forget I am showing now.

Chelle   I have that . . .

Louise   People don't often ask actually /

Chelle   . . . I forget that other people can see / [it]

Louise   They see the uniform but not . . . I forget that I am showing now. That people can see now.

Beat.

It's normal. Baby kicking you.

Chelle   Actually that wasn't what /

Louise   It's perfectly normal.

Chelle   But that wasn't what I was, it's how I *feel* when /

Louise   It's good. It's good that baby is moving about /

Chelle   It was how it makes me feel when he does that. When he kicks me.

Louise *starts to apply the monitor to* **Chelle**'*s wet belly.*

Chelle He kicks me all the time.

The monitor lights up. **Chelle**'s *baby is on the screen.*

Beat.

Louise There he is.

Beat.

Miss Culliford?

Chelle What?

Louise On the screen.

Chelle *doesn't look at the screen.*

Chelle Yes.

Louise (*indicating*) Just there.

Chelle I can see.

Louise OK.

Chelle OK?

Louise Yes.

Beat.

I was just checking.

Beat.

Chelle OK. Sorry.

Louise Lovely baby, a lovely healthy baby. Isn't he lovely?

Beat.

Would you like a picture?

Chelle A picture.

Louise You can have pictures to take away with /

Chelle Have you got one?

Louise   They're nice to have. You can show them to people.

Chelle   I said have you got a /

Louise   You can show people your baby. You could show your . . . your /

Chelle   I'm fine thanks.

Pause.

Louise   It said in your notes that you are still . . . Michelle /

Chelle   I know /

Louise   In your notes that you haven't managed . . . that you haven't managed to give up the smoking yet.

Chelle   I know /

Louise   Has your GP spoken to you . . . he has probably spoken to you about how important it is for baby to /

Chelle   I have been told and I do know.

Beat.

Louise   Well I could certainly, if you like, I could certainly give you some leaflets.

Beat.

I know how hard, how hard it can be for some women, some women find it very hard. You shouldn't feel, no one is judging you Michelle /

Chelle   Yeah /

Louise   No one is going to judge you.

Chelle   Yeah.

Louise   Some women take to it like /

Chelle   Right /

Louise   Being. Pregnancy /

Chelle   Right /

Louise   Like ducks to / water

Chelle   Like you you mean?

Beat.

I was going to call it Seren.

Louise   That's /

Chelle   If it was a girl.

Louise   That's lovely /

Chelle   It means star.

Louise   Really lovely /

Chelle   Anyway it's not a girl so. I'm not having a girl. It's a boy, so I won't be calling it Seren.

Beat.

I'll remember him.

Louise   Sorry?

Chelle   I'll remember him. I don't need a picture. I'll remember him.

Chelle *looks at the screen; they look at it together.* **Louise**'s *hand moves to her belly once again.*

Five

Early morning, the office is still in half darkness. **Clive** *is in the kitchen area, standing by the kettle. As we enter the kettle is boiling, the noise is loud and there is a lot of steam.* **Clive** *pours the tea into a cup. He watches the cup.* **Stella** *enters behind* **Clive**.

Clive   Tea?

Stella   I . . . I . . .

Beat.

I don't drink tea.

Clive   Suit yourself.

Beat.

Stella   Milk and two.

Clive   I thought you said you didn't . . .

Stella *half shrugs.*

Clive *gives* **Stella** *his tea and starts to make up a second cup.*

Stella *takes the tea but doesn't drink, she is trying to get the courage to say something.*

Stella   You're really good at it.

Clive   Sorry pet?

Stella   It's just I, when I am doing all the paperwork, all the, your, the paperwork /

Clive   The wrap /

Stella   Sorry, yes, the wrap, I knew that, I knew what it was called /

Clive   Doesn't / [matter]

Stella   So silly of me though because I did know . . . the wrap, the wrap, the wrap . . .

Beat.

But I noticed . . . what I noticed is that you always check that the customer has got exactly what they want before you ring off . . .

Clive   I talk too much.

Stella   You make sure they have got exactly what they need and I just think that that is . . .

Clive   I keep the customer on the line and that holds up the queue and that means that our, I drag the waiting time, the time customers have to wait on the line before they get answered gets dragged up because of my tendency to talk. Madge is always having 'little chats' with me about it.

They both sip their tea for a moment.

I like it when it's like this.

Stella   Me too.

Clive   Before anyone arrives.

Stella   After the cleaners have gone.

Clive   And everything is all so . . . so . . . empty.

Beat.

Stella   When I come in, when I come in in the morning I notice that the air feels, which is silly really, a block this big, with this many companies there must be lots of people who have come in before me, but it feels. Feels.

Clive   Like it is completely untouched by people /

Stella   Like no one has ever /

Clive   Like I am alone here in the /

Stella   Like this is a forest, a rainforest that no one has ever, has ever been to before and /

Clive   Exactly, exactly, like virgin rainforest and I am the first person to have been /

Stella   And you are the first person ever to /

Clive   Me cutting through the undergrowth in a pith helmet /

Stella   Silly, but the first person to have ever touched this.

Beat.

Clive   The heavy weight of the air on my scorched back and mosquitos buzzing round my neck and with only, only me and the machete that I am using to hack through, hack my way through the dense undergrowth. The darkness of shadows all around and threatening to engulf and the ever present, the really ever present danger that snakes or a lion or a gorilla will bite me through and send me, me . . . the stink of the forest floor threatening to engulf me at any moment.

Beat.

Because it is normally just me in my pith helmet and my machete hacking through, the wires from the telephones like fast growing, really supernaturally fast growing vines threatening to cut me down where I stand any minute and by the ankles drag me across the beige sea of newly hoovered carpets and deposit me feet first in the shredder, in the paper shredder that Madge normally uses to dispose of confidential documents.

Stella   I'm sorry to interrupt / [your]

Clive   It's normally just me in all that. But it's nice having you here now.

They sip their tea.

Because the thing is, the thing is about all that, about all this here.

Beat.

The thing is that I was thinking I might get a dog.

Stella   Lovely.

Clive   Teach it tricks, take it for walks, pet it.

Stella   Really lovely.

Clive   But if I got a dog I wouldn't be able to come in here this early /

Stella   I hadn't /

Clive   Because you couldn't bring a dog in here /

Stella   I hadn't thought of that /

Clive   It would be cruel. It would be cruel to bring an animal in here really. And anyway, I probably wouldn't, because it would need taking for walks, feeding and taking for walks and so I wouldn't be able to come in here early any more.

Beat.

Because I love, because over the break, over the holidays, over Christmas I did, I did miss that. I did miss this /

Stella   I love that. I love that about this here /

Clive   And even if the waiting times are long and I am not, because I do have the tendency to just – as Madge says to just drift, just drift off, I do. I do love this here. The stillness and that. And that is why I am not, I am not at all sure about this dog even though I do think that it would be lovely /

Stella   Because why would you ever want to give this up? /

Clive   Be lovely to have something to look after like that. But I just think that this here, this forest /

Stella   Why would anyone ever want to give this up? This silence and the sound of the rainforest humming like this. Why would anyone choose to give this up?

Six

The sound of rain on glass. The office. **Madge** *is sitting at the staff kitchen table with some papers in front of her.* **Stella** *is sitting opposite. In front of her there is a glass of water.*

Madge   The Caribbean, the Bahamas, Seychelles, down to Morocco, and up the Nile. You should drink that water.

Stella *drinks the water.*

Madge   Dresses covered in sequins, legs up to here, behind like a greyhound and a real, a proper bosom. Not like these saggy things I have now, flop flop flopping against my belly like old balloons. It was magnificent, my bosom. Enough to make grown men weep.

Beat.

I would sing in those dresses and Liza Minnelli you know, like the diva herself. On one occasion we went up the Norwegian fjords and it was the first cruise of that kind that we had done, that anyone had done really. It made us feel, well I suppose we were in a way. Unique. Because we normally went south of course, to the heat and the warm waters, which was always, to be honest, was always the bit I struggled with. That heat beating down on the back of my neck all day and sweat collecting in the creases in the back of my knees. I want to see you drink the whole thing before we start please Stella.

Madge *eyes* **Stella** *as she continues to drink the water.*

On the second day of the cruise one of the dancers, Pam, I think her name was, was standing in the restaurant by the buffet provided gratis for all guests and staff (and a very good spread it was too) when she suddenly, all of a sudden she lurched forward, violently, as if thrown, as if picked up and pitched forward and prostrated on the floor as if praying and she vomited.

Stella *sits forward slightly, dizzy.*

Madge   Are you going to /

Stella   No /

Madge   Are you sure that you are not going to throw / [up again]

Stella   I'm fine now, it was just a . . . I just felt dizzy all of a sudden and . . . and . . .

Madge   Because I will, as Team Leader, if you do again I will have to send / you

Stella   No.

Beat.

Madge   It's company policy Stella. I wasn't asking your /

Stella   I promise I won't.

Madge   I wasn't asking if you wanted to.

Beat.

Because you could make the whole team, before you know it the whole team will be contaminated, your being ill will have *contaminated* the whole team.

Stella   It's the strip lighting I think.

Madge   The whole ship was sick Stella.

Stella   Or maybe it's the air conditioning /

Madge   The whole ship, everybody on it /

Stella   Or something /

Madge   It's not a nice thing to say, to think about even but just. Just. Awash with vomit, rolling around on the water with everyone vomiting.

Stella   I'm sorry /

Madge   Don't be sorry /

Stella   No, no I am /

Madge   Don't be sorry /

Stella   I am /

Madge   Don't be *sorry* Stella but if you are sick I will have to send you . . . I will have to send you home from the office.

Beat.

It is just policy. It is out of my hands. It's just, it's policy.

Stella   I feel fine now. I promise I won't be sick again. I feel fine now.

Madge   Well. We'll see won't we?

Stella   Yes.

Madge   We will see. We will see if you are OK. We will see if you are fine.

Beat.

Sometimes people think that because of my age I might be a soft touch and I do certainly have quite a lot of sympathy and time for the people I am in charge of here, I do care about them /

Stella   You have made me feel /

Madge   And I am, as I say, a kind of mother /

Stella   That is exactly, that is exactly what I /

Madge   A mother figure. I am in fact a mother and so I would say naturally enough I have become a kind of mother figure to those who work with me here. Work with me here on my team.

Beat.

But at the heart of the thing /

Stella   You have, you have become like a kind of / mother to [me]

Madge   You do, you come here to do a job /

Stella   A kind of mother to / [me]

Madge   That might sound brutal /

Stella   With this being my first job, my first time away from home and me being all . . . all, my being on my own I . . . I /

Madge It might sound 'insensitive' or perhaps a bit
brutal but /

Stella I /

Madge Because I am not actually your mother Stella /

Stella I /

Madge Because you do (I expect) you do probably have
your own mother /

Stella I /

Madge Your own mother whose job it is to take care of you.
To phone you and check how you are and make a fuss of you
on birthdays and at Christmas. To care for you and nurture
you. To look after you and take an interest in how you are,
emotionally as well as physically. I expect you do have
someone like that in your life?

Stella I'm.

Beat.

I'm not that close to my mum actually.

Madge That is sad. That is sad. But. But, and nevertheless.
But nevertheless and however I might feel about that
personally, I am an employee, just like you and I am here to
get the best out of you (from you) for the company. As an
employee. So I must. I think we must get on with your
appraisal mustn't we?

Stella Yes.

Madge If you are feeling quite alright?

Stella Yes, of course Madge.

Beat.

Madge I have to tell you that the company really does
really regret how long it has taken us to arrange this review /

Stella That's OK.

Madge   I'm glad you think so /

Stella   I do, it's fine /

Madge   But it actually isn't, it isn't OK because you should not have had to cope on your own this long without reflecting on your progress.

Stella   Right.

Madge   It's just that with the staff shortages, with the cut-backs and the staff shortages this is the first time I have had a chance to sit down with you like this.

Stella   I see, I /

Madge   To sit and reflect like this on your progress in your first four months with us.

Beat.

Because in these recessionary times we cannot afford any slack, we cannot afford any dead wood in our company, in this, our corporate family.

Beat.

But nevertheless, nevertheless I can tell you that you have performed very well in your first few months with us here at Scion Communications.

Stella   Have I? Have I really Madge?

Beat.

Madge   You know, you know, when I was on that boat. When I was still a cabaret singer on a boat on a cruise on crystal clear, that azure blue water, those huge glacier formations, those icy walls of rock and the rolling green of the land beyond, I started to get sick.

Stella *stands unsteadily.*

Stella *runs to the sink, leans over.*

Madge I threw up. I threw up every morning for a week.
The girl I shared a room with thought that I had that virus,
the bug that I was telling you about before, that was going
around the whole boat and making people really very ill.
But it wasn't that at all. Because at first I just vomited, but
then my belly and my breasts swelled and I started to get
these, this kick kick kicking in my gut, I got it all day and all
night, this incessant kicking, bruising up of my insides and
soon I couldn't fit into the dresses any more, the beautiful
jewelled dresses that I had to wear when I was performing.
(**Madge** *goes over to* **Stella** *and rubs her back, holds back her hair
as* **Stella** *vomits into the sink.*) Because as I said I hated that
heat, the heat of the sun coming down on me and the feeling
of being continually too hot. Too hot and never able to get
cool. It made me feel uncomfortable and so, in the end it was
not really all that terrible that I had to come home. That in
the end I had to come home and have my little Harry. In a
way it was the best thing that could have happened to me.

Stella *vomits again.*

Madge Because I had had a very long and very successful
career as a very glamorous singer on those boats, those
cruises and so really at that time I was ready and so it was
probably the best thing that could have happened. The very
best thing.

Seven

*The great swooping, fluttering of wings as birds flock together.
Migrating. A bedroom. Early. A double bed and bedside table with
baby monitor and* **David**'s *mobile.* **Chelle** *and* **David**'s *clothes are
tangled together on the floor.* **David** *is asleep in the bed,
spreadeagled.* **Chelle** *(no longer pregnant) is sitting on the edge of
the bed, dressed in a large T-shirt, palms to eyes. She draws her legs
up under her T-shirt. A moment. She drops her legs heavily. She
picks at the hair at the back of her head. The sound of a baby*

beginning to grumble on the baby monitor. **Chelle** *lunges to switch it off, knocking it to the floor awkwardly.*

Chelle   Fuck.

Chelle *turns the baby monitor off.*

David *stirs.*

David (*looking at his mobile*)   What time / [is it]

Chelle   He'll be a nightmare now /

David (*reading the time on the display*)   Christ.

Chelle   He'll start screaming in a minute.

David   Thought we set the alarm.

Chelle   He won't go back now. That's it now. He's up.

David   I thought I remembered us setting / the

Chelle   For the rest of the day now /

David   I thought I remembered setting it last night /

Chelle   Because he was up twice in the night /

David   I was on the edge of sleep when / I had that feeling . . .

Chelle   He woke me twice in the night and so he hasn't actually slept properly and now he is up and he is going to be cranky all day now.

Beat.

I had to feed him. Mum was meant to get up with him last night but she slept through so I had to do it. I had to get up and do the night feed /

David   I had that sensation, when you are just on the edge, and your heart leaps and your arms and legs fall away from you like there is nothing under them /

Chelle Him sucking on that bottle like a pig, like a little suckling pig /

David Like you are about to fall, like you are about to drop, about to fall off the edge of the world.

Beat.

Chelle You kicked me /

David And then you jolt, you jolt awake /

Chelle Kicked me in the thigh.

David Your whole body jerks. Like a shock. An electric shock. Right to my fingers. I rolled over, rolled over on my side, on my left side, puffed if I am honest and spinning away from you and I could have sworn I set the alarm, the alarm on my phone for six-thirty.

Chelle I'll probably have a bruise.

David I set it.

Chelle I bruise like a peach.

David Do you think I dreamt it?

Chelle What?

David Do you think I dreamt setting the alarm?

Chelle Why would you / dream

David Because it didn't go off but I definitely remember setting it /

Chelle Can't have /

David Right.

Chelle Can't have set it can / you?

David Right. No.

Beat.

David *gets out of bed and starts to put his trousers on.*

Chelle   I was that far gone.

David   Yeah?

Chelle   I was that rat arsed.

David   Have you seen my watch?

Chelle   I was that bladdered I wouldn't have known if we had set the alarm /

David   I left it /

Chelle   I wouldn't have known if we had set the alarm or /

David   I must have put it /

Chelle   Whether we set the alarm. What you said or what we did. I can't really remember what we did.

Beat.

David   Can't you?

Chelle   That was how fucked I was.

Beat.

David (*picking up his watch from the floor*)   You have mascara under your eyes.

Chelle   It's meant to be waterproof.

David   On the tops of your cheeks.

Chelle (*taking a pack of baby wipes and starting to wipe her face*)   It's meant to be waterproof but it's not.

David   Right.

Chelle   They never are.

Beat.

David   Have you been crying?

Chelle   What?

David   It's just it looks like you've been crying.

Chelle   Mascara smudges if you leave it.

David   Does it?

Chelle   Didn't you know that?

David   Why would I?

Chelle   Thought I had been crying because of what?

Beat.

David   You don't need it.

Beat.

The make-up.

Chelle   I wear it all the time.

David   You look fine without it.

Chelle   I wear it all the time /

David   I'm just saying /

Chelle   You've never seen me without it. You have never seen me without my make-up so how would you know if I need it?

Beat.

David   Haven't got it on now.

Chelle   Don't be a dick David.

Chelle *scrubs at her face harder.*

Beat.

You seen Madge's new admin.

David   Sorry?

Chelle   Madge's new admin / assistant

David   I hadn't /

Chelle   Yes you have. Administrative Assistant lass on Madge's team.

Beat.

David   New girl on Madge's team /

Chelle   You know who she is.

David   Oh . . . Stephanie.

Chelle   What?

David   Her name.

Beat.

Chelle   How d'you /

David   Interviewed /

Chelle   Right /

David   Interviewed her didn't I.

Beat.

Chelle   Twenty?

David   What?

Chelle   About twenty.

David   What?

Chelle   Her age.

David   I don't know.

Chelle   But roughly?

Beat.

David   Younger I think.

Beat.

I don't know.

Chelle   Must have been on her form.

David What?

Chelle When you interviewed her. Must have been on her application.

David Don't have to put it. Not meant to actually. Advised not to and we aren't meant to give the candidate the opportunity to tell. To tell us her age, verbally or in writing. Could lead to discrimination.

Chelle So you are saying you don't know?

David It's better that we don't know.

Chelle *starts to get dressed.*

Chelle But she's probably younger than me?

David I don't /

Chelle Younger than me anyway.

David I didn't really notice how old / she was

Chelle But you don't really know. Don't really remember her so you don't really know.

Beat.

Have you thought about how you are going to get to work?

David Christ.

Chelle Takes ages on the /

David How do you get in? /

Chelle Takes ages on the bus /

David Is that how you /

Chelle Mum drives me.

David Right.

Chelle We drop Rory off at the daycare.

David (*looking at his watch*) Right.

Chelle   And then she drives me into work.

David   Going to be late.

Beat.

Chelle   You going to give me a warning?

David   What?

Chelle   If I am late again you going to give me a warning?

David   That wasn't what I meant.

Chelle   Because actually I have already had a warning because I have actually been late twice in the last month and this will be the third time and then I won't qualify for the bonus, the annual bonus that is distributed amongst all employees (and it probably seems petty to you but) all advisors of my level at your centre if I am late again.

Beat.

Madge told us, she said that that was the position.

Beat.

David   You know that that wasn't what I meant.

Chelle   I'm only joking with you.

David   Right.

Chelle   Can't you take a joke?

Beat.

I didn't think you would want to /

David   What?

Chelle   Turn up with me.

David   Oh /

Chelle   I would have offered you a lift but /

David   No it's /

Chelle I would have offered but. People seeing us turn up together.

David No /

Chelle People might get the wrong idea /

David No, I'll just /

David's *phone goes off, he looks at it.* **Chelle** *looks at him. He decides not to take it.*

(*Distracted.*) I'll get a taxi.

Chelle Of course you will.

David What?

Chelle Nothing.

David What?

A baby starts to scream off stage.

Chelle Told you. Little bastard. He'll be a nightmare all day now.

Eight

The office. Morning. **Clive** *is standing in the kitchen area. His hand is bandaged, but a little blood has started to seep through and* **Stella** *is re-dressing it with items from a green First Aid box that is open next to them.*

Clive Because the thing about yer Doberman Pinscher is that he matures slowly, he's a big dog and he grows slowly and in proportion with his slow physical growth his capacity to learn things, his mental capacity is also, he evolves that mental capacity (and he is a clever dog) at a slow rate. Very slowly. He is what, if he was a human we would say that he was a late developer. Which is quite appropriate really because I was also a late developer. Took me ages to learn to read and then, well, it wasn't until much later that I really valued, really understood the *value* of education so you could say that James /

Stella   James?

Clive   That's his name. The dog's name. It's James. So you could say that James takes after me.

Beat.

So I spent all weekend just teaching him this one command /

Stella   All /

Clive   Just this one command over and over again /

Stella   All weekend? /

Clive   My wife, my Louise, she /

Stella   Must get tiring /

Clive   She laughs at me, she says, 'Clive what a fucking waste of time, what a fucking waste of time' /

Stella   You must get tired /

Clive   'What a fucking waste of your time Clive.'

Beat.

Point is he wasn't. It was like he didn't have a clue, all weekend I am just giving this one, just this one, from eight a.m. to five p.m. /

Stella   Must have been really frustrating /

Clive   And to be honest I am beginning to wonder /

Stella   You must have begun to think /

Clive   If he will ever, if he will ever /

Stella   Begun to think, what is the / [point]

Clive   And then all of a sudden it was like something. Something clicked /

Stella   Clicked?

Clive   Something clicked /

Stella   Clicked. /

Clive   In his head and just did the trick straight off. No fuss, just like that /

Stella   That's /

Clive   Like he had just worked something out. Just figured something out in his head and now he understood.

Stella   That's brilliant.

Clive   So we did it, we did it two more times, in the garden, in my back garden, just, I was so pleased. I can't tell you how pleased I was /

Stella   What was it?

Clive   Sorry?

Stella   What was the trick?

Clive   Oh. I taught him to play dead.

Stella (*finishing dressing the wound*)   There.

Clive   Do you have any pets?

Stella   No.

Clive   No pets?

Stella   No, not, not at the moment.

Clive   That's a shame.

Beat.

Stella   When I was little I had a rabbit.

Clive   Oh yeah.

Stella   I had a lovely pet rabbit called Sasha.

Clive   Lovely.

Stella   I would watch her every day after school, squat down on the gravel with the sun on my neck poking bits of vegetables through the bars.

Clive   That's lovely.

Beat.

Stella   And after a while I noticed she had patches missing from her fur. Little patches of skin all exposed and pricks of blood like a shaving rash so I watched her. I watched her all afternoon. All evening. As it got dark the white fur showed up against the blackness and her sharp little teeth as she pulled the fur out of her own skin. Great tufts of white fur. And that night. That night when I was meant to be asleep I woke up with a jolt because she was screaming. Screaming so loud and I didn't know that rabbits could do that, could scream like that. I went down to the hutch in the morning and she had given birth to a litter of rabbits.

Clive   They make nice pets.

Stella   They do.

Clive   And it's good for a little girl,

Stella   Exactly,

Clive   Especially a little girl – to have something,

Stella   Something to care for,

Clive   Especially for a little girl and this might sound,

Stella   Because that is the thing about pets isn't it,

Clive   Probably does sound a bit old-fashioned,

Stella   That is the thing about them,

Clive   That's what Louise doesn't understand. She doesn't understand that. Understand how important that is, to have that sense of purpose, of responsibility, of power to nurture something even when you are only, are actually only a powerless, a powerless little girl.

Nine

Early summer. Frogs croaking loudly. A fire exit outside the offices.
David *and* **Madge** *are standing in the smoking area. They are both*
smoking.

David   They had painted, had painted the second bedroom
a sort of sickly pale yellow colour and he said that they used
it mainly as an office now and there was a desk and all his
papers, this bloke's papers, all over the desk, on all the
surfaces, stacked high in piles on the floor and it was a right
mess. Kirsten said, whispered to me when he was in the
other room, 'He needs to get himself a filing system. A
decent filing system and tidy up all this crap before he shows
people round the house,' and she did have a point. It was a
state. I looked out the window which claimed to be south-
facing only it wasn't, wasn't at all, Kirsten used an App on
her phone that she had downloaded and it was only south
west, not south at all and you could see over everyone's
gardens, over all the back gardens, and fair game it was
quite. There was something quite beautiful about it. About
that, all these people's gardens, all these people . . . and
there was this boy in a tree in the garden opposite and one
across and he had a sword, had this plastic sword and he was
sitting in this tree, hitting it again and again and shrieking,
every time he hit the tree he let out this enormous shriek like
a fox or something and every time he hit it all these leaves
and blossom, all this blossom fell off. Floated down. Like
confetti or something.

Beat.

Kirsten asked later, asked the wife later, 'Do you get much
noise from the neighbours?' and she claimed not but then
she would wouldn't she. She would say that.

Beat.

We got three mortgage offers in the end /

Madge (*putting her cigarette out*)   Even now and in this climate /

David   Three! /

Madge   When it is almost impossible to get on the /

David   Impossible to even get started on the property /

Madge   When it is almost impossible to get your foot on the first rung of the /

David   Of course Michael did kindly, he did kindly offer to pay for a deposit /

Madge   Which is why you need family to /

David   He did kindly offer to help us out . . . he said he would be happy, he would be happy to do it /

Madge   Because that is what family are for after all. That is why you have family, to get you started, so you can start your family and so on and so on and so on just like that in that exact same way and each generation giving way to the next like that. Each giving way to the next like that.

Beat.

David   But it wasn't really for us though.

Madge   No.

David (*putting his cigarette out*)   Not really for us in the end.

Madge   No.

David   Because you aren't meant to move in late spring.

Madge   'Course not.

David   In early summer, you are meant to wait. You are meant to wait until the winter to get the best bargains. And anyway with Kirsten just being made manager her mind.

Madge   Such a beautiful, successful couple.

David   With her now the manager of that whole store, of that whole flagship store at one of the nation's leading clothes stores she has other things on her mind.

Madge   Only natural that you would want to take the next /

David   She has other things to worry about.

Madge   But just not yet eh? Not quite yet /

David   She has bigger fish to fry at the moment.

Beat.

And anyway, like he says, as Michael says it's not, and I am not old-fashioned, I'm not traditional but it is not the normal thing is it, to buy before you, you are meant to wait until after you have, until after the wedding really, to buy a house together. That is the time to buy a house together.

Madge   When are you . . . have you I mean, have you set a date?

David   You get engaged, you get married, you buy a house and then you think about, that is when you start to think about starting a family.

David *looks at his watch, moves slightly.*

Beat.

I should probably . . . time to get on really. I should probably get on.

Beat.

It's a shame though.

Madge   Sorry love?

David   What you told me /

Madge   Oh /

David   What you just said /

Madge   Should probably /

David   About /

Madge   Because she did tell me in confidence but /

David   About the admin / girl

Madge   But I thought as her Line Manager and since you are my Line Manager. I thought I probably, probably had to tell you.

Beat.

David   She was good wasn't / she

Madge   Very efficient /

David   Very good at her job /

Madge   Best we have /

David   And pretty too /

Madge   Best admin lass I have /

David   She was pretty /

Madge   Most efficient admin lass I have /

David   She was pretty too. Could have done better for herself.

Beat.

Madge   She won't tell me who he /

David   Could have done better than /

Madge   I tried to coax it out of her /

David   Because I sometimes wonder /

Madge   Tried to get her to tell me /

David   It's not politically . . . whatever /

Madge   Because we are close, me and /

David   But you employ these young women and /

Madge   We are quite close and I thought that she might /

David   I said to Michael /

Madge   Oh /

David   I wasn't, of course I didn't name names /

Madge   No /

David   And I didn't know that Stephanie /

Madge   No . . . of course / [not]

David   At the time I didn't know this was her position, but only the other day I said to Michael, I said I sometimes think that they should be made to sign something /

Madge   I thought that she might tell me who he was. Because he should /

David   A waiver or something to say /

Madge   He does have /

David   'I will not' /

Madge   He does have the right / to know

David   'I will be here for more than five minutes' / . . .

Madge   The father. He has the right to know that he has, that he will have a child, he will have a baby in a few months and that, that responsibility I suppose.

David   'I will be here for more than five minutes before I get myself impregnated by some prick from accounts.' He laughed pretty hard at that I don't mind telling you because it might not be, alright granted and in this day and age, because of course women have as much right to work, to be here as the, and you know that about me Madge and excuse the, but as much right as the next man, but you do get to the point where . . .

Chelle *enters, holding a packet of cigarettes.*

Beat.

Chelle   Oh . . . I was just /

Madge   It's alright Michelle /

Chelle   Because it was, it is my /

Madge   Me and Mr Thwaite were just /

Chelle   Right /

Madge   Just going back in weren't we David?

David   Yes.

Madge (*to* **Chelle**)   Just five minutes though Chelle.

Chelle   I know /

Madge   Just five minutes for a cigarette break Michelle that is all /

Chelle   I know /

Madge   That is all you are allowed. Because you need to be careful Michelle, two lates already this month and three the last, you need to make sure that you are keeping on top of your timekeeping.

Chelle   I'm just having my break.

Madge   Just make sure. Just make sure that you are not becoming lax that is all I am saying Michelle. I don't want to have to dock your bonus again. (*To* **David** *as they go towards the door.*) I'm sorry David, you were saying /

Chelle *goes over to the area with the cigarette stubs. She stands, fiddling with her hair, and clicks the lighter in her palm repeatedly, waiting for them to leave.*

David   Because you get to the point where you think they should be made to sign something /

Madge   Exactly /

David 'I will not fucking shag some prick from accounts and end up up the duff and on the maternity before I have even.' /

Madge (*laughing*)   Exactly David /

David 'Before I have even earned my keep' /

Madge   Very naughty of you but I know exactly /

David 'Earned my right to be here in the first place.'

Madge   You naughty, naughty man David! /

David   He laughed pretty bloody hard at that I don't mind telling you. Michael laughed pretty hard at that, no mistake.

David *opens the fire door for* **Madge**.

It begins to rain.

Pause.

Madge   It said it would rain, thunderstorms later it said. I'm quite pleased.

Madge *steps towards the door.*

David *is staring at* **Chelle** *now. Almost unconsciously,* **Chelle** *looks back.*

David   He looked such a terror, that little boy in that tree.

Madge (*looking out*)   Quite pleased. Clear this dreadful heat.

David   Looked such a little terror. Such an absolute little terror. A right little tyke.

Madge *and* **David** *exit.*

Beat.

Chelle *lights her lighter, but she is holding it too tight and she has to light it three times before she can get it to sustain a flame to hold to a cigarette.*

Ten

Clive *and* **Louise**'s *kitchen. A breakfast bar. The French windows are open. The sound of barking.* **Clive** *enters through the French windows. He puts a small dead frog on the breakfast bar. Its entrails are all messed. Perhaps a little blood. He shuts the French windows. He wipes his hands on a tea towel. He looks at the frog. The sound of the outside door being opened and shut.*

Louise (*off*)   Clive.

Louise *enters. She is not pregnant any more. She is wearing a nurse's uniform with unseasonable woollen tights. She is carrying shopping. She notices the frog.*

Shopping.

Beat.

In the car.

Clive   Right.

Clive *exits.*

Louise *pauses, looking at the frog.*

Clive *enters holding more shopping.*

Louise *starts to put the shopping away.*

Louise   Window is still stuck on the driver's side.

Clive   Is it.

Louise   Jammed.

Clive   Should get that fixed.

Louise   Told you about it before.

Clive   Should get round to it.

Louise   Yes.

Clive   I will.

Louise   Couldn't hardly breathe.

Beat.

Felt I was suffocating.

Beat.

A frog in a pan, in the traffic with the window jammed, rolled up, full of simmering water. All the way to the shops. A pan of simmering water and the frog just sitting there. Just sitting there in the car. The temperature gets turned up and its insides start to cook. Start to boil from the inside with the heat.

Clive I'll fix it.

Louise I could feel my thighs prickling.

Clive This weekend.

Louise My feet stuck on the pedals in my hot shoes and my tights. Boiling and the smell of the hot plastic from the dashboard.

Beat.

It's meant to get hotter this week. Meant to get even hotter than it is already.

Clive I said I'll fix it.

Louise Will you?

Beat.

I need to take my tights off.

Louise *takes her tights off.*

My thighs.

Beat.

Did you take him for a walk?

Clive Of course.

Louise Where?

Clive   All over.

Louise   To the Moor?

Clive   All over the Moor. Leazes Park.

Louise   Did you let him off /

Clive   As soon as we were in the park took the lead off /

Louise   Straight away?

Clive   There weren't any children.

Louise   None?

Clive   During school hours /

Louise   No little kids?

Clive   No /

Louise   Babies /

Clive   No /

Louise   But you don't know.

Clive   There weren't.

Beat.

Louise   Still.

Clive   What?

Louise   The other people in the park.

Clive   Other dog walkers.

Louise   I always wait until I am in that top field.

Clive   Do you.

Louise   As a courtesy to the other people in the park /

Clive   A courtesy /

Louise   The other people who might not like dogs /

Clive Christ /

Louise Did you throw him a /

Clive I threw him a ball. He fetched it. I threw it in the pond. He swam after it. He ran around, he barked at three other dogs.

Louise Did he?

Clive Yes. Quite loudly. It echoed about.

Louise Weren't you /

Clive He was only playing really.

Beat.

Louise I hate it when people say that.

Clive What?

Louise 'He's just playing', 'He is just being playful' /

Clive He is though /

Louise 'He wouldn't hurt a' /

Clive He wouldn't though. He wouldn't hurt a fly.

Beat.

Louise Because you hear about these dogs all the time /

Clive Not our /

Louise Dogs that go wild suddenly /

Clive Not our James /

Louise Go completely mad. Go completely mad and attack their owners.

Beat.

Attack their owners, bite them, draw blood. Make them bleed.

Beat.

Clive   No /

Louise   And sometimes they /

Clive   No he /

Louise   You hear how they go completely mad and attack children /

Clive   James would never /

Louise   Disfigure little children. Just suddenly go completely mad and disfigure tiny children.

Beat.

Clive   Just playing. He was just playing. Yapping and barking at the other dogs, chasing /

Louise   Chasing?

Clive   Yes, chasing each other. Like they do. Like dogs do. Playing. It's what they do.

Louise   Please stop saying that.

Clive   What?

Louise   'It's what they do', 'It's just what they do', 'It's perfectly normal'.

Clive   Well it is, it is perfectly normal.

Beat.

Louise   Did he go to the toilet?

Clive   He shat in the car park.

Louise   Clive.

Clive   Big shit. I had to get a shopping bag from the boot.

Louise   Clive.

Clive   What?

Beat.

Louise   Did you give him his food?

Clive   Of course I did.

Louise   Well.

Clive   I looked out, looked out the window half an hour ago. He was sat on the patio. Just sat panting, pant, pant, pant, on the patio.

Beat.

Louise   Did you see him /

Clive   What?

Louise   When he got the frog in his mouth, when he /

Clive   Of course not /

Louise   Did he tease it, did he tease it like last /

Clive   I don't know.

Louise   He always plays with them. That's what I don't, what I can't . . . he plays /

Clive   You thought I would watch him doing that. Watch our dog /

Louise   Your dog.

Clive   Whilst he killed it.

Beat.

Louise   You haven't asked me.

Clive   What?

Louise   My first day.

Clive   I was going /

Louise   My first day back at the hospital.

Clive   I was going to.

Louise   Were you?

Clive   I was about to.

Louise   All you wanted to talk about was that stupid dog.

Clive   I was going to ask you.

Louise   There was a woman came in. She was bleeding.

Clive   You just, you didn't give me a /

Louise   We had to give her a sedative. She stopped crying after that.

Beat.

My face is hot. It's burning up, I can feel it. My cheeks. It's too hot in here. I need to open a window.

Eleven

The office. Morning. **Chelle** *is looking at herself in her compact mirror. She pulls a face. Starts to reapply foundation furiously.* **Stella** *is standing nearby watching.*

Chelle   So I just smacked it on you know, just slapped it on really.

Stella   You sit across from me /

Chelle   I was late and I was rushing /

Stella   Hunched forward and headset on and sometimes /

Chelle   I was trying to do a million things and I wasn't concentrating /

Stella   Do you recognise me? /

Chelle I just slapped my make-up on this morning so now I am having to redo it /

Stella   Do you recognise me at all though Chelle?

Chelle   What?

Stella   I was just asking if you /

Chelle You sit across from us.

Stella Yes.

Chelle You are the new admin girl.

Stella I've been here for eight months now.

Chelle Yeah.

Stella I've been here for quite a while.

Chelle But you do the admin.

Stella Yes.

Chelle You took over from Sharon.

Stella Did I?

Chelle Didn't you know?

Stella I'm Stella.

Chelle She used to do your job, now you do it.

Chelle *looks at* **Stella** *briefly.*

I was rushing and I had a million things to do and so I wasn't, I wasn't really concentrating so now I am having to redo it.

Chelle *goes back to looking at herself in her compact mirror.*

Stella I watch you sometimes when you are on the phones. Headset on and your forehead tipped forward, you concentrating on what you are saying and tap tap tapping at the computer.

Pause.

Why do you pull your hair out?

Chelle (*looking up*) What?

Stella Sorry, just /

Chelle You been watching me /

Stella   No. I just /

Chelle   You been spying on me /

Stella   I've noticed that you pull hair out the back of your head /

Chelle   You have been watching us, looking at me all the /

Stella   I just, I noticed and /

Chelle   I can't believe you were watching /

Stella   I just happened to notice /

Chelle   You just sitting there watching me like /

Stella   No, it wasn't like that . . . I just noticed.

Beat.

Chelle   Well no one else has.

Stella   Haven't they?

Chelle   Everyone else leaves us alone.

Stella   No one has ever noticed before?

Chelle   I get these hairs that are thicker than my normal hair and they grow crooked and I /

Stella   You pull them out.

Chelle   I like all my hair to be the same. To sit the same way. That's all.

Chelle *continues to apply her make-up, ignoring* **Stella**.

Me and Shazzer used to get slaughtered together.

Stella   What?

Chelle   Me and Shaz.

Stella   Who?

Chelle   Christ. Keep up. Shazzer – Sharon. Girl you took over from. We were good mates.

Stella Were you?

Chelle Used to go out, go out of a Friday after work, straight out of work and down the Quay before you could /

Stella What?

Chelle Before you could say happy hour. Two for one on the vodka tonics.

Beat.

Got to enjoy yourself while you can haven't you /

Stella Yeah.

Chelle Young, free and single.

Stella Yeah you /

Chelle Got to enjoy yourself before you get tied down.

Stella Yeah you got to /

Chelle Because it all goes to shit in the end doesn't it?

Beat.

It's funny that you should mention Shaz /

Stella Shaz?

Chelle Christ. Are you slow or /

Stella Sorry. I, my head feels a bit . . . bit . . .

Chelle What?

Beat.

Admin support girl, because she used to be a right laugh. She used to be a real giggle and then she brought in these photos one day, these pictures and then before you knew it was an endless bloody stream of these fucking endless fucking photos of this blob, just this blob, this growing blob and she gave up smoking, gave up drinking, gave up fucking everything and then all she would talk about was the fucking blob. Like it was the most important thing in the world.

Beat.

You wanna go for a drink sometime Stell?

Stella   A drink?

Chelle   Cheeky pint after work?

Stella   I would love /

Chelle   Go out, Friday night down the quayside and get rat arsed. Get actually bladdered?

Stella   I would love that.

Chelle   She wasn't going to breastfeed or nothing cos she wanted, she *needed* to be able to go out again she said, she was going stir crazy sat at home with it and she said she couldn't wait to get back, get back to work, to vodka tonics and the odd frisking in the disabled loos and to me, her best friend, and the fun we used to have together here in the office and out on the lash.

Twelve

The office. **Madge** *is knitting some yellow wool.* **Stella** *has a Tupperware box with a sandwich in it. She has lost her appetite.*

Madge (*holding up the knitting.*)   Do you like it?

Beat.

Stella   I . . . Madge . . .

Beat.

I . . . because I did want to talk to /

Madge   It's for my Harry /

Stella   To talk to you actually Madge /

Madge   It's going to be for my Harry /

Stella   Because I got your email, I got your email that you sent to everyone /

Madge   My Harry's little boy /

Stella   About my party for me here at Scion.

Madge   And you know, on his birthdays I always used to make a cake, every year, like clockwork and one year, one birthday I made him a cake like a shark, because him and his dad used to go fishing so he wanted a shark cake so I made him one, made this great cake shaped as a shark, took me hours. All covered in Smarties and with red licorice for its big fishy tongue curling out on the foil-covered board that I had used which represented the sea /

Stella   Because you have . . . you've invited everyone actually haven't you, the whole office /

Madge   And now we do everyone's birthdays /

Stella   You . . . you sent it to everyone /

Madge   We do all the birthdays here and it's not /

Stella   And I . . . I . . . I . . .

Madge   It's not the same obviously as my Harry and his cakes that I would make by hand, I would make personally and by hand every birthday. Obviously it's not, not the same thing, but we do try. We do try to do everyone's birthday.

Beat.

We used to sing but it became a bit unmanageable. With the numbers, the numbers that work here now. Even with the cut-backs I mean because people would sing 'Happy Birthday' and then maybe they would cheer and say hooray and then people, we found that people were more chatty than normal after that, they would joke and talk loudly. Not that there is a problem with that, not that we are saying that people cannot *talk*, but it is really about creating the wrong atmosphere, the wrong environment. So now we just gather for the cake and a cup of tea. We don't sing any more. Because at the end of the day it's an office, it isn't a social club.

Beat.

But with this /

Stella   Because I wanted to say that I really don't /

Madge   With you it's /

Stella   I don't want you to go to any /

Madge   It's different with a baby /

Stella   I don't want you to go to any trouble because I don't . . . I don't, if I am honest, I am not sure that I /

Madge   Because with the quality testing season coming up and everyone is feeling . . . and it is understandable really and you must /

Stella   Because I am, obviously I am grateful /

Madge   And you must sense it, in the office, in the, all the teams you must sense that yes, there is an element of /

Stella   But all this attention, the attention being all on /

Madge   Because we all, we all need to get those waiting times down don't we? Get those call times and the waiting times down and get those customer satisfaction figures up up up because they are not, because last year we did not, and this is no secret Sarah, but we were, we did not reach near the /

Stella   What did you /

Madge   Near the top of the company and I know that you do not /

Stella   What did you call me? /

Madge   Because at the end of all that, the stress of all that we need . . . and you are a kind, sensible girl and I am sure that you know . . . what we need is to have that, that party for your baby to look forward to.

Beat.

Stella   Yes and I do /

Madge   I knew you would /

Stella   I do understand /

Madge   A chance to gather round, to gather and have a few drinks and all of us all together /

Stella   I do understand what you are saying Madge, it's just /

Madge   And some eating and some drinking and perhaps some, perhaps a bit of a dance and all of us looking at you, really admiring your lump, your growing bump, the new life that you are bringing into this world. Us all taking time to admire that.

Beat.

Stella   I do of course, but, but, but . . . because I haven't . . . I haven't told everyone /

Madge (*laughing*)   But they must . . . they must /

Stella   I haven't told everyone about the. . . about it so /

Madge   They must be able to see. I mean they must be able to see. Just look at you. Look at the size of you. You are practically. You are practically blooming.

Stella   I just /

Madge   Yes love?

Stella   I.

Pause.

Madge   You must feel, well, overwhelmed with it /

Stella   Exactly /

Madge   You must feel completely overcome with that /

Stella   I do, I do Madge, I feel completely, like what you are saying /

Madge   Because you are bound to feel overwhelmed /

Stella   Because I'm not, I'm not even sure if I am, if I am blossoming /

Madge   Yes . . .

Stella   If I am opening up, if I am ripe with that, with what you say I am /

Madge   Yes.

Stella   And so if I have this party where everyone can see that /

Madge   Yes /

Stella   Can see that blossoming that you say you can see then I don't, I don't know what that would /

Madge   Yes /

Stella   What that would mean /

Madge   Yes /

Stella   What would it mean Madge?

Madge   Yes /

Stella   What it would mean for me here at the office, if I was about to . . . If I was going to . . .

Madge   Yes, yes, overcome with the beauty of it.

*Pause, in which **Madge** continues with her knitting.*

Madge *smiles at* **Stella** *who has started to cry.*

Madge (*about the knitting*) It's a blanket. It's yellow because when he was born my daughter-in-law didn't want to know, she wanted the surprise I suppose. I don't know. I don't know why she didn't want to know the sex, but she just didn't. So I knitted him a yellow rabbit, a yellow jumper, tiny yellow boots and so I will knit him this blanket and I will put it in a packet and I will send it to Australia and my daughter-in-law will put it in his cot. His cot or. He probably sleeps in a bed by now. And he will lie there and he will think about his English Nana. His English Nana who doesn't like the sun and his English Granddad who likes Fry's Turkish Delight. And even though we have never met he will think of us. Me and his Granddad. His Granddad who might not. Who doesn't actually remember about him any more. Doesn't remember him or his Daddy or the cakes that I used to make and he will think of us when he is lying under that blanket at night. Even though his Granddad does not remember him and I cannot . . . because of the distance and the heat and how I hate flying anyway . . .

Beat.

So you must let us, allow us to celebrate that. Because it's about our family, it's about all of us. This Scion party for this Scion baby is going to be about all of us.

Thirteen

The slightly malevolent sounds of insects in a rainforest and the heaviness of hot air familiar from wildlife films morphs into the spinning of fans and the clicking of the broken air conditioning machine. It is late morning, the office is too warm and there are makeshift fans that people have brought from home. **Chelle**, **Madge** *and* **Clive** *are on the phones. They have headsets on and are typing on screens.* **Madge** *is finishing a call.* **David** *stands over her desk waiting for her to ring off.*

Madge (*looks at* **David**, *smiling, as she speaks into her headset, she logs out on her keyboard at the same time*)   . . . and thankyou very much for ringing us sir, once again Scion Communications on behalf of Hotpoint Electrics do apologise for the inconvenience caused. Have a good day.

Madge *pushes her chair back from her desk. We see she has kicked her shoes off and has her skirt hitched.*

I know, because I do know, believe me David I do know what you are about to /

Clive   Can I ask you to give me the first line of your address please /

Chelle   Just the first line of your . . .

Madge   I know what you're going to say /

Chelle   Road or /

Clive   Is that the full /

Chelle   If I could ask you to spell /

Madge   I know what you are going to say.

David   Because I know how much pressure you must all feel under but /

Chelle   Thankyou /

Madge   And I do appreciate that David /

David   I know how much I feel under and so I can only assume that that effect has trickled down to you all but /

Madge   I appreciate that you have thought about that but I do know that it is just not really good enough.

Clive (*readjusting his headset*)   Is that better, can you hear me better now /

Chelle   Thankyou and postcode?

David   But our figures (and you know as well as I do) that our figures have continued to be pretty, well to be honest it has been a pretty lacklustre performance and our wrap times have so far and unless things pick up in the next week have been / pretty poor

Chelle   Your postcode /

Clive   Can you hear me now, yes /

Chelle   Yes and we will get to that but if I could just ask you to give us your / postcode

David   As have the call times and so despite fairish customer satisfaction figures our centre will come in sixth overall out of nine in terms of the whole season, and that's not /

Madge   It's not really good enough is it David.

David   Six out of nine in terms of efficiency and call volume so /

Madge   I completely understand that it is just not really good enough and at the team meeting I did lay it down /

Clive   Can you hear me better now madam?

Madge   I did lay out the problems quite comprehensively to my team and /

David   Good /

Clive   Good. So what was it that you /

David   Good Madge.

Beat.

Clive   I am sorry to, I am sorry to hear / that

Madge   I said that to them this morning that while I do know how hard it is to work in this sort of heat at the end of the day that is not an excuse for the situation that we now find ourselves /

David   And goodness knows it is not just about my position /

Madge   The heat in this office should not be an excuse for the position that we now find ourselves in. And of course for you, your being, it being your . . . This being your family /

David   Because it is actually not about how I might feel about this personally but /

Madge   Your personal business in a way, your family /

David   Goodness knows it is not just *my* job that is on the line.

Madge   So it must feel so terrible to have all that on the line.

Beat.

But if you offset those who score better in customer satisfaction against the sheer speed that /

Clive   That it must have been, yes, must have been very difficult with this awful heat and /

Chelle   I understand that madam and I am just going to ask you to tell me precisely what the problem with the cooker is /

Clive   I know, I know, and /

Chelle   Precisely how long /

David   Yes /

Clive   I would say /

Chelle   I'm not /

David   Yes /

Clive   That yes we have had /

Chelle   Shall we say forty-five minutes then?

Clive   There has been a particular problem with that model overheating.

Beat.

That has been quite widely reported, yes.

David   Because I do appreciate that the heat problems, and we are trying to get them sorted but /

Madge   But it has been, and there is no getting round this, the conditions that we are working in, with the air con still on the blink and us having to bring in our own fans from home and of course, you know us David, we always pull together in times of /

David (*loosens his tie*)   Because it should not be slowing us down to the extent that it has /

Chelle   I just need to put a round number down madam. I just need a number for that.

David   It should not, it should not be affecting our productivity to this /

Madge   And we do all try to pull together but /

Clive   The heat seems to have tripped something in their /

Chelle   I'm afraid I cannot tell you /

Clive   In their circuits and . . . Yes I think it is yes unfortunately quite a widespread /

Chelle   I am not able to tell you if it is a currently, if it is a widespread /

David   So we have to, I know it is harsh /

Madge   I under / stand

David   I know that it seems like a harsh thing /

Madge   I am right behind you David /

David   But we have to /

Madge   Because we are /

David   Call time is key and while we are doing better /

Madge   Much bette / r

David   A bit better in respect of customer / satisfaction

Chelle   And anyway I don't, I actually don't know so /

Clive   I know /

Chelle   No /

Clive   I know /

Chelle   No . . . so I cannot /

Clive   Yes, I do, I do absolutely understand / how . . .

Chelle   I'm afraid I can't comment on that.

David   Because like Michael says and above everything we cannot allow the customers to bleed all over the place into what should be wrap time and to bleed their problems all over us, to bleed all their woes all over this call centre, letting the customer and all their many myriad of problems bleed all over our open-plan office into all the cubicles and into everyone's work stations, on to everyone's keyboards and whilst I know that the, I understand that the air con is, yes, is yes, might have an impact in how *compassionate* the advisors are able to, how well they might be able to score in that specific capability /

Madge   They cannot allow how they feel to be communicated /

David   It is not actually necessary to sympathise too much with them anyway /

Madge   They must not communicate that feeling, the feeling they have in this office of being too hot, too hot and never able to get cold over the phone /

David   It is much better for the customer if we can just deal with the problem and move on. Just move on.

Clive   Because I have little ones myself /

Chelle   Because madam, because, do not, do not, I should warn you madam /

Clive   I have little ones so I can yes /

Chelle   Do not raise your voice at me madam because I will yes, I am going to put you on hold madam whilst I get a Line Manager to deal with you . . . your complaints /

Clive   I have little ones myself so I can quite understand madam.

Chelle   Madam? Madam? Madam? . . . Shit.

Chelle *sits back on her seat for a moment, plucking at the back of her hair, and then begins to type up her notes from the call.*

Clive   And thankyou very much for ringing us, once again Scion Communications do on behalf of Hotpoint Electrics apologise for the inconvenience caused. Have a good day.

Clive *logs out of the call and starts to write up his notes.*

David   Because like Michael says, 'There is, this might sound a bit harsh but it is, as much as anything else it is about efficiency, because the thing is efficiency *is* good, it *is* good customer service after all and like I am, like I am always saying I did not – no – I did not set up, I did not go into this business thirty years ago (and I am a self-made man David and do not forget that) and build this house that you are standing in and buy those four Japanese cars that are sitting out there on that driveway and afford the three foreign holidays a year that have given me this beautiful chestnut brown tan and I did not bring up my three gorgeous daughters who have been, have all been as you know David, have all been privately educated, and are in fact delightful David. I did not do all that by listening to people tell me their . . . because this business is not a counselling

service, it is not a bloody counselling service David, it is a
customer call centre and that is what we are here for.'

Madge *turns back to her computer, still smiling at* **David**, *and logs
back in.*

Chelle   Hello Scion Communications / how can I help you?

Clive   Hello Scion Co / mmunications how can I help you?

Madge   Hello / Scion Communications how can I help
you today?

Fourteen

*The office. It is night. It is silent. There is the kind of low-level
lighting that is left on when large offices are not in use.* **Stella** *is
standing on something high up. She looks around her.*

Stella   Hello?

Beat.

Hello. Hello you are through to Michelle Culliford. You are
through to Michelle, to Clive, you are through to Margaret
at . . . at . . . at . . . Edexcel. At Northampton Banks. At
Hotpoint Electrics. May I help you today. I. I. I. That must
be. That is. Something that we are. We are aware, we are
aware of that. The company is. Do you have a pen . . . a pen
. . . (*More carefully.*) a *pen.* Yes. Handy. If I could just stop
you. (*Changing.*) I've taken ten this. It is. It is. I know it isn't
even. It isn't even a *joke.* I just. I put her on. I put her on
hold and. Maybe that will be a. That might be a. Hopefully
she will fuck off. Yeah exactly fuck off. Yeah exactly fucking
fuck off. Yeah (*Laughs.*) yeah I know. I know. My feet are
killing me. My head is *killing* me. It is *killing* me.

Stella *hears a noise off, panics, tries to get down too quickly and
slips, hurting her hand slightly. Perhaps there is a little blood.*

Chelle *enters. She is on her mobile.*

Chelle   Yeah. No. I'm still here Mum. I.

Stella *is standing, visible to the audience and to* **Chelle**.

Chelle *does not see* **Stella**.

Chelle *picks up her handbag that she has left on her desk.*

Beat.

Yeah. Just finishing my shift. Always takes me a bit to. I don't know. I don't know Mum. I know. I told you remember and you said. Yeah and you would look after him tonight. No. Yeah so. Drinks with the lasses so. Yeah. I have to have a life Mum so. And. Exactly.

David *enters. He watches* **Chelle**.

Chelle   Kid or no kid.

Chelle *sees* **David**, *smiles tightly, mouths 'sorry'.*

Exactly. Right Mum. Right. I'll see you in. Yeah. Bye.

Chelle *hangs up.*

David   Drinks with the 'lasses'.

Chelle   You don't get to judge me David /

David   Again /

Chelle   You don't get to be . . .

Beat.

Cos you know how she feels about /

David   Alright Chelle /

Chelle   How she feels about you.

Beat.

Cos when was the last time you saw Rory /

David   What?

Chelle   Rory. When did you last come to see him?

Beat.

David   Why are you talking about Rory all of a sudden?

Beat.

Chelle   Because he has really, his hair and his eyes and something about how he is now. He is starting to look. Look like /

David   What has Rory got to do /

Chelle   He is actually quite handsome now.

David   What has he got to do with this?

Beat.

Chelle   I am actually, me and Stella are going /

David   Stella?

Chelle   Admin lass.

David   You're going where /

Chelle   Friday night, we are going down the /

David   You're going out on the lash with Stephanie /

Chelle   You jealous?

David   What?

Chelle   Jealous of me / or of

David   Girl from Madge's /

Chelle   Which one of us are you jealous / of

David (*laughing*)   Pregnant girl from Madge's /

Chelle   Which one David?

David   Because Madge said that she was /

Chelle   We are actually having a session on Friday so actually I was telling the truth in a way. To me mum, just now I mean.

Beat.

I was sort of telling the truth.

David   But Madge said that /

Chelle   Jesus, that woman is such a gossip /

David   She said that Stephanie was / pregnant

Chelle   Bollocks.

David   Because they're having a baby shower.

Chelle   You do chat some absolute shit David.

David   I said, I did say that with the figures the way they are maybe now wasn't the best time for a party but you know Madge, you know her, stupid old cow, once she has decided /

Chelle (*taking a step*)   You hear that? /

David   Once she has got an idea in her head.

Chelle   That.

Beat.

David   What?

Chelle   Scratching noise.

David   Electrics.

Chelle   A scrabbling.

David   Probably the electrics. Air con and that. It creaks a bit sometimes, that's all.

Chelle *is listening again.*

Chelle *moves to another part of the office.*

Chelle *picks up a paper guillotine carefully, trying not to make any noise.*

Chelle *squats down slowly with the guillotine, listening.*

Chelle *swings the guillotine repeatedly and brings it down again and again with regularity and precision on something in front of her.*

Chelle *stops.*

Beat.

Chelle *stands up.*

David   Christ Chelle /

Chelle   Its leg is still twitching but /

David   Bit /

Chelle   They do that. It's the muscles contracting or spasming or something. Doesn't mean they are alive.

David   Bit brutal /

Chelle   What would you have done?

David   Seemed a bit violent /

Chelle   I was trying to kill it.

David   Most women would have /

Chelle   What?

David   Stood on the table and screamed or /

Chelle   Like you did you / mean

David   I didn't /

Chelle   Wanted to though.

Beat.

The way you looked at it, like you wanted to run or /

David   The way you went at it like that /

Chelle   You want our office to be /

David   Like / you

Chelle   Your office that you manage. You want to have it overrun with mice? Because it would be. Because they manage to scratch their way in to somewhere, in somewhere nice and damp and warm, warm like the office /

David   Yeah alright Chelle, I've told you that we are getting the air con fixed so /

Chelle   And they will breed and breed and breed until there are hundreds, literally hundreds all crawling over each other with their grey oily skin and their fleshy pink tails and their little claws scrabbling inside walls /

David   I have told Michael how important it is to get it fixed so /

Chelle   Because they could shut you down, health and safety, having an infestation, being overrun like that, they could shut you down. Because you don't want that do you, for your company, you cannot want this all to come crumbling down like that because of a little mouse?

Beat.

Maybe me and Stell will rock up at Her Madge's desperate little party /

David   Do you think that is /

Chelle   Maybe we will rock up and show you lot how fucking slaughtered we can get.

David   Do you really think that is a good idea Michelle?

Chelle   Kids or no kids.

Beat.

Ready to go?

David *and* **Chelle** *leave.*

Stella *stands for a moment.*

Fifteen

Twilight. **Clive** *and* **Louise***'s kitchen.* **Clive** *is facing the French windows. He has mud and petrol up his legs and on his hands. There is a little blood on his hands. The clicking of a lighter. It clicks a number of times and we see* **Clive***'s face lit up in it. He looks tired and his face is dirty.* **Clive** *puts his hand to his chest, up his neck, leaving a long oily streak.* **Clive** *lights the lighter once more, watches it burn, holds it to the palm of his hand. He does not react to the pain.* **Clive** *looks out the window again.* **Louise** *enters, she is barefoot. She looks as if she has been crying.*

Louise   Clive.

Clive   I fixed the car window.

Beat.

You were right. It does get very.

Louise   Clive, where have you . . .

Beat.

Have you been to the park /

Clive   Like a furnace /

Louise   Or on the Heath or /

Clive   Like an oven in there. I can see what you meant now. I was driving back and I pulled up on the drive and I was just sat there, just sat there for a minute on the drive in the car to get my breath back and it started to make me feel . . . felt anxious, that heat makes you feel anxious so I thought, get it done now, do it and then it's done.

Louise   Thankyou. Thankyou Clive. That's great . . .

Beat.

Where have you been though?

Beat.

Because it has been . . . you've been out for hours and I was
. . . I was getting . . . I was getting quite worried.

Beat.

Clive   I'm going to a party tonight. Back at the office.

Louise   You didn't ask me if I wanted to go.

Clive   I didn't think you would want to.

Louise   You didn't give me a chance to decide.

Clive   Sasha is having a baby.

Louise   Who?

Clive   She's having a baby and tonight we're having a party.

Louise   Who is?

Clive   Girl that I work with. Sasha.

Beat.

Louise   You could have told me /

Clive   I didn't think you would /

Louise   You could have /

Clive   I didn't think that you would want to /

Louise   I'm not . . . I'm not a /

Clive   You haven't met her /

Louise   I can look at a pregnant /

Clive   You haven't met so I didn't think that /

Louise   I see pregnant women every day Clive.

Beat.

You don't need to . . .

Clive   I didn't want you to feel awkward because you hadn't
met her before.

Louise   Clive.

Beat.

Clive   That dog. That mongrel. That beast.

Beat.

Because he did bite me /

Louise   I need you to listen because I've been to /

Clive   He bit me /

Louise   Because we said we would go to the doctor's /

Clive   He bit me all the time /

Louise   And now I have / been

Clive   He snapped at my fingers /

Louise   I went today while you were out /

Clive   He would snap at my fingers and growl at me /

Louise   And I sat there in that chair, opposite him and he had put out an extra chair because they always do don't they and we do the same and I thought about all those women that I see every week who don't have someone with them when we turn on the monitor, when we look at the baby for the first time and as he told me I looked down at my hands, my knuckles, the whiting of my knuckles where I was gripping, really gripping my knees and I looked at his face, and he has a sort, a sort of kind face doesn't he, that doctor, a kind face, and I remembered how kind he had been last time, how nice he had been to both of us and I was sat there on that plastic chair next to that other plastic chair like I said, just looking at his kind face and I just wanted to smack him Clive, I had to really clench my fists on my knees, my knuckles almost see-through now with the effort stopping myself from smacking his stupid face Clive.

Clive You were right about him. About how he hurt me and made me bleed so I thought, get it done now, do it and then it's done so I did it: I fixed the car and I fixed that too.

Louise Clive are you listening to what I am saying, what I am telling you?

Clive You shouldn't wait up.

Louise (*trying brightly*) We are going to have a baby Clive!

Clive I might be back quite late so you shouldn't wait up.

Clive *leaves.* **Louise** *looks out over the garden, places her hands on her belly protectively.*

Sixteen

Chelle's *bedroom.* **Stella** *is standing in the middle of the room in a tight stretchy minidress.* **Stella** *has a small baby bump that was not really visible under her office clothes before this point.* **Chelle** *is sat on the bed. She is wearing a short skirt too. They are getting ready to go out. In front of* **Chelle** *there are two glasses. She is carefully measuring out spirits. 'Don't Stop the Music' by Rihanna plays.*

Chelle That drink with the smiley lemon on it (*She grins.*) gurning. Really. Like (*She grins again, harder.*)

Stella Feels tight.

Chelle Kind of drink you can only drink when you are fourteen really. Grinning hard. Aggressive that lemon was.

Stella Does it look tight?

Chelle Meant to.

Stella It's making me sweat under my arms.

Chelle When monkeys show their teeth in the PG ads. It was that sort of grin.

Stella It's still got a stain.

Chelle Where?

Stella (*indicating*)   Coke or /

Chelle Doesn't show.

Stella But you can see it.

Chelle Doesn't show unless you point it out. Unless you are going to point it out to people. Are you?

Beat.

Stella No. But /

Chelle Means they are aggressive when they do that. People think they are smiling but they aren't. It's aggressive.

Stella I feel like I am /

Chelle Last time I wore that I was fourteen.

Stella (*touching her belly*)   My belly feels like it's sweating.

Chelle Can't believe it's been ten years since I wore it.

Stella Like wearing bandages.

Chelle You're tiny.

Stella It's that tight.

Chelle Like a child really.

Beat.

Two bottles I had. Head on the ceiling, looking down. Fourteen years old and my head is on the ceiling.

Stella Floating /

Chelle First time I have had a drink. Room is spinning below me, I'm looking at my mates and my Britney posters and my head is on the /

Stella You had grown wings or . . .?

Chelle Right.

Stella   Imagined that you had.

Chelle   Well, yeah /

Stella   You imagined that you could float.

Chelle   In Oceana /

Stella   You felt you could float up.

Chelle   After two bottles and half a tab on the bus /

Stella   Like the air was beneath you and the room was spinning away from you and /

Chelle   Dancing in that dress and this bloke grabbed at the elastic near my knickers.

Stella   Like a balloon on a string /

Chelle   Grabbed at me /

Stella   You were floating in the air and pulling you back /

Chelle   His sausage fingers /

Stella   Like he was trying to pull you back down from the ceiling /

Chelle   Big sausage fingers pulling at my knickers /

Stella   And him, him smiling at you /

Chelle   My tiny, me tiny and his . . . him so big. Him so big and these sausage fingers.

Beat.

Pressed myself up against him, me up against him and grinding. Me grinding him.

Chelle *picks up the glasses, downs her own glass and gives one to* **Stella**.

Stella *holds the drink uncertainly.*

Chelle *starts to dance, grinding up against* **Stella**.

Stella   His hands at your waist and his mouth opening
slightly, as his face tilts forward and you can feel that he has
pushed you up, up against the desk and the white light, that
white winter light streaming in through the big glass
windows and his body up, up close against yours, thin office
shirt and new shoes, the squeak of your new shoes against
the desk leg and the sweat collecting in the back of your
neck, your knees and his arms up round you, his mouth /

Chelle   Because it was boiling in there /

Stella   Because it is just a bit too hot in here so you can feel
the sweat collecting /

Chelle   And he is pushed up against me /

Stella   In the creases in the back of your neck, your knees /

Chelle   Smell of him /

Stella   Because he never got the air con, the air con in here
still isn't working and you are feeling like you are boiling,
literally boiling /

Chelle   His erection /

Stella   Boiling like frogs.

Chelle   His erection pressing in the small of my back.

Chelle *stops grinding.*

Stella   But he is off you now. His hands gone from under
you and he is off you. Off across the office like he is floating,
floating on air like nothing happened. Like it was nothing.

Beat.

Chelle (*about the dress*)   I can't get into it any more.

Stella   I feel like I am suffocating /

Chelle   I can't even get it over my hips /

Stella   Like the dress might be /

Chelle I have this. That one day I will just get the bread knife /

Stella Like I might actually be /

Chelle The knife that I use every day to cut the bread and I will just slice it off.

Stella Like it might actually be suffocating me.

Chelle Slice that fat off my hips.

Stella Like this might be suffocating me Chelle.

Chelle Because I used to wear that dress all the time but then I got . . . I had /

Stella Chelle /

Chelle I put on weight and now I don't wear it any more /

Stella Chelle. I needed to talk to you /

Chelle I get it over my head and then I can't /

Stella Because this party, the party that we are going to /

Chelle I get my arms into it but then /

Stella The party at the office /

Chelle I can't get it over my breasts, over my belly. I am that fat now I cannot get it over my fat belly.

Beat.

Tonight I want to get /

Stella Chelle /

Chelle I want us to get off our faces /

Stella Chelle can I ask you /

Chelle And I want to get completely bladdered /

Stella I need to ask you something and /

Chelle I want everyone to see how pallatic I can get.

Stella   Because I don't know. I don't know if I . . . I don't
know if I even want it. If I even want this party. I don't know
what I want. What I am meant to want. I want you to tell me.
Can you tell me Chelle? Can you tell me what I am meant
to want?

Beat.

Chelle   You going to drink that then?

Stella   What?

Chelle   What I just give you Shazzer.

Stella   Oh.

Chelle   I want to see you drink the whole thing. I want to
see you drink the whole thing before we leave.

Beat.

Stella *drinks the shot.*

Seventeen

*The introduction to Petula Clark's 'Downtown' plays loudly. Tail end
of the party: the desks have been pushed back as far as possible, there
has been some attempt at decoration and there is quite a lot of food
and drink half eaten and lying around in patches.* **Madge** *is
standing by the karaoke machine in a sequined dress holding a
microphone.* **David** *stands nearby, holding a beer.* **Chelle** *is
watching them both.* **Clive** *is sitting, he is still wearing the same
mucky clothes from scene fifteen. He holds a lighter.* **Stella** *is sitting
some distance apart from the others. They have all been drinking.*

Madge, *singing, dances towards* **David**. *As she approaches the end
of the first verse there are tears in her eyes. Her singing grows in
confidence towards the climax of the chorus, and as the instrumental
section kicks in* **Madge** *holds* **David**'s *gaze:*

Madge   '. . . AND YOU MAY FIND SOMEBODY KIND
TO HELP AND UNDERSTAND YOU, SOMEONE WHO

IS JUST LIKE YOU AND NEEDS A GENTLE HAND . . .'
(*She touches* **David**'s *face in a motherly fashion.*) '. . . TO GUIDE
THEM ALONG . . .' (*She withdraws her hand, getting louder.*)
'. . . SO MAYBE I'LL SEE YOU THERE . . .'

Madge *concludes the song, singing it out loudly.*

As the music fades out she kisses **David** *full on the lips.*

Christ you look just like my Harry.

Chelle What?

Clive *lights his lighter.*

Madge My Harry. David looks just like my Harry.

David Do I?

Clive *is watching the flame on his lighter.*

Madge I didn't see it before but you are the absolute spit of
my Harry.

Chelle I don't think so.

Madge She hasn't met him. (*To* **Chelle**.) You haven't you
know love.

Through the following **Clive** *lets the flame go out and holds it to his
hand.*

Chelle I've seen pictures.

Madge What?

Chelle Photos. On your desk. He doesn't look like your
son. He's got paler hair.

David You've got some voice there Madge.

Clive *lights his lighter again.*

Madge Thankyou. I trained.

Clive *lets the flame go out.*

David Oh yeah?

Madge   On the boats.

Chelle   Did you?

David   Right pair of lungs on you.

Madge (*to* **David**)   Flatterer. I'm not what I /

Chelle   Cos you never, barely ever mention / it

Madge   Flattery will get you /

David   It's the truth.

Madge   I used to have a beautiful voice but I haven't used it for /

David   Well it doesn't show Madge.

Madge   Haven't used it for so long and I'm so out of practice now that /

David   It doesn't show at all.

Madge   Because I trained on the boats when I was very young /

David   It's like you never stopped Madge /

Madge   But then I had, I fell pregnant with my little Harry and I cannot (*Laughing.*) I cannot tell you how angry I was with that baby, because I was only twenty-two and still at the height of my powers in terms of my singing and my looks and my general, my general joy for life and I had the whole of my life ahead of me really but then I fell pregnant by a local lad from back here and so I had to come home and you cannot imagine how exploded, how eviscerated I was by that baby, by my little Harry!

Together:

Madge *laughs again.*

Clive *lights his lighter again, watches the flame.*

David   Well I thought you sounded just beautiful.

Clive *lets the flame go out.*

Madge   But you can't stay, can you, after you have a little person like that in your life, you cannot stay angry with them for long can you and he did, he does, he still melts my heart David.

Beat.

(*Smiling widely at* **David** *and taking in the whole room warmly.*) I just have to say /

Chelle   Christ.

Madge   What was that Michelle?

Chelle   Nothing Margaret.

Beat.

Madge   I do actually, I have actually prepared a little . . . just a little.

Beat.

I have actually prepared (*Beginning to well up.*) a little. A little speech.

Beat.

Shall I . . . David should I?

David   Go on.

Madge   You sure?

David   Go on Madge, I am sure that we would all /

Madge   The others might not want to hear /

David   'Course they /

Chelle   Can hardly wait.

Madge   Will I go on then?

David   You go ahead Madge.

Madge *takes out a small piece of typed paper from the neckline of her dress.*

Madge   OK. So. So here we are.

Beat.

Here we all are together, gathered for such an auspicious gathering. All of us all gathered on this auspicious occasion and so I thought I might, friends and colleagues, I thought I might talk to you about how I might, or you might, how we all might spend our day here at Scion Communications. So here is what my day, here at Scion might be like: I might arrive fifteen minutes before the shift begins and normally Clive is normally already here, he is normally stood over there by the kettle, and of course this is not an exact science, because sometimes I am a couple of minutes early or I might have got stuck in traffic, but Clive normally already has the mugs out ready and has popped the kettle on to boil. Then Chelle and Pat and Debbie arrive. We all have a gossip, who did what at the weekend. Who is starting at the centre. That sort of thing. We will work and then at lunchtime I will go to Boots to get the Meal Deal with Pat and she will tell us about her angina or complain about her sons who are both driving her mad or her husband who is a bit ill, but she will make light of it, because she always does, she makes light of it even though her husband has been in and out of hospital recently. Normally Rick will put on the kettle at about three when we are all starting to flag and he will crack some stupid joke, some silly joke, often quite, often a bit rude actually and then, before you know it's five-thirty and I am off home. Off home. And then it all starts again the next day.

Madge *puts the piece of paper back in her cleavage, maybe wipes away a tear.*

That is what I wanted to say and that is why I wanted to celebrate this auspicious occasion here with you. My team. My family. The people I treasure. I have come to treasure the most and that is why . . . why I . . . why we, why me and

Sarah wanted to spend our special day here with you, in this office with the people that we love.

Everyone applauds.

Would you like to say anything lovely?

Pause.

Stella   I . . . no . . . I

Madge   Don't be shy /

Chelle   Yeah don't hold /

David   You go ahead /

Chelle   Don't you hold back now.

Stella   I . . . I . . . I don't feel . . . I feel like I am not quite sure what you want us to . . . what it is that you want us to . . . I, I . . . I . . .

Beat.

Thankyou . . . thankyou for this . . . for all this.

David, **Madge**, **Chelle** *and* **Clive** *all clap.*

Madge   That was /

David   What a lovely /

Madge   How lovely /

Chelle   You going to say anything David?

David   What?

Beat.

Chelle   You got anything to say our esteemed leader?

Madge   Yes David, you should.

David   I . . . I . . .

Madge   You should say something.

Chelle   You must have something to say.

Madge   Go on David.

Beat.

Chelle   You should have something to say about our . . .
because despite all this and Madge's lovely speech you must
have something to say about /

David   I . . . I . . .

Chelle   About how badly our centre is performing.

Beat.

Because I am pretty sure that my score, what was it Madge?
I am pretty sure that my score was pretty pissing poor, pretty
fucking pissing poor and especially on protocol /

Madge   Oh Michelle, I don't think that this is /

Chelle   You always bring it up in my review Madge and you
are quite right of course. I have a tendency to say whatever I
am thinking and that goes, that often definitely goes against
the protocol, the agreed script that we all have to read from
when we, when the advisors, us lowly advisors have to abide
by when we answer the phone doesn't it?

Madge   I don't think that this is something that we should
be talking about now / Michelle

Chelle   I tend to lose my temper and just, to just blow up
sometimes on the phones, if there is a / difficult caller

Madge   Maybe we should talk about this later Michelle /

Chelle   Must make you want to say something to us
though? About what that poor performance means for us all
David? Madge?

Madge   I think we should talk about this another /

Chelle   But I suppose the thing is that I am working on it.
I'm working on my motormouth. I am learning to rein it in
aren't I Madge? I am learning to shut the fuck up.

Beat.

My turn next anyway.

David   What?

Chelle   My song.

Beat.

I've been practising haven't I?

Madge   I didn't know that you /

Chelle   Didn't you?

Madge   No.

Chelle   Well I do. I'm like you Madge. I love singing. Singing is my life.

Madge   Well that is /

Chelle   Isn't it? What we've been doing together, all those nights when Rory /

Madge   Rory?

Chelle   Because me and Shazzer, me practising /

Madge   Who's Rory?

Chelle   And her listening while my big booming voice comes crashing out my mouth and sometimes I do feel a bit bad for leaving my poor little fatherless bastard boy with his Nan but then I think, I just think that noise that I can make that comes out of my mouth is so *glorious*, just so *glorious* that actually it is worth that sacrifice, because at the end of the day, at the end of the day when all is said and done it is just. It is *glorious*.

Beat.

I need a drink first though. Before I sing. I need a drink.

Beat.

Madge   I don't think you should /

Chelle   What?

Madge (*to* **David**)   You're not going to / [let her]

Chelle   What is it Madge?

Madge   David?

Beat.

I don't know what it is that has upset you Michelle but as your team leader I have to say /

Chelle   What do you think David?

David   Well I think you probably have had /

Madge   I am your team leader Michelle /

Chelle   David?

Beat.

Madge   David has already told you what he thinks Michelle and as your team leader I am telling you again. You can't, I am sorry to be a . . . to put a dampener on it, but I think you have probably had enough.

Chelle (*to* **David**)   You going to stop me having a well-deserved drink Mr Thwaite?

Pause.

David   Well I suppose it is a party /

Madge   David /

David   And I know you want this to be a good evening /

Madge   Well yes . . .

David   That is what we all want.

Madge   But don't you think that Michelle should go easy . . .

Beat.

David (*holding up a bottle of spirits*)   Why don't we all have one? One final drink before we all hit the road eh Madge?

Madge   Well . . .

David   Go on Madge . . .

Madge   Go on then Mister Smooth. Twist my arm.

David *tops them all up.*

Madge (*to* **Chelle**)   What are you singing then?

Chelle   What?

Madge   What song are you going to sing Michelle?

Beat.

David   I'll sing with you if you like Chelle.

Madge (*laughing*)   You don't need to do that David!

Chelle   I don't want you to /

David   If you want me to sing with you Chelle, I am just saying /

Madge   Oh David, you absolute charmer.

Chelle   You are a charmer David.

Madge   Isn't he a gentleman Chelle?

Beat.

David   I don't mind singing with you Michelle.

Chelle   You're alright.

Madge   Lovely of you to offer David.

Chelle   I can do it on my own. I want to do this on my own.

Chelle *takes the microphone from* **Madge**, *leans down and selects a song on the karaoke machine. They all watch her. Through this we can hear* **Stella**'s *breathing becoming irregular and shallow.* **Chelle**

stands up and looks directly at **David** *expectantly. The opening bars of 'Hit Me Baby One More Time' by Britney Spears.* **Stella** *bends over in pain. Everyone is looking at* **Chelle**.

Together: **Chelle** *opens her mouth to start singing.*

Stella's *waters break.*

Stella *screams.*

Clive *sees* **Stella**.

Clive (*shouts*)   Louise!

Eighteen

David *is standing on a ladder by the air conditioning control box in the office. The air conditioning is not working and every four or five seconds it can be heard loudly trying to start up, the lights flickering as it does so.* **David** *has sweat patches under his arms and on his back.* **Stella** *is standing at the foot of the ladder. He has not seen her. She is no longer pregnant.*

Stella   It always was /

David   Christ /

Stella   It always was temperamental wasn't / it . . .

David   Christ! Fuck . . . Christ. Gave me a. Nearly gave me a /

Stella   That air con /

David   Nearly had a heart attack /

Stella   It was always overheating. It would make your thighs stick together, your hair plastered to the side of your face and then you would get these patches, these dark moons of damp under your arms, on the back of you and at your crotch /

David   Stephanie?

Stella   It would make you feel /

David   Stephanie? /

Stella   Would make me feel quite unwell. The heat bearing down on me and the still still air because there is no – without it there is actually no natural ventilation in here at all is there. It is actually completely sealed in here / without it

David   How did you . . .

Beat.

Because you cannot . . . you cannot just come in . . .

Stella   Sealed like a Tupperware box without it /

David   You do not work here any more so you cannot just march in here and . . . and . . . and . . .

Stella   Us all sealed in here inside a Tupperware box sweating and sweating.

Beat.

I smiled and the girl who was leaving just smiled back, she smiled back, in that automatic way when someone smiles at you you just smile back, it's not personal of course it is just. You can't help it. It's automatic. Like a dog.

Beat.

She pushed the door open, and smiling back, I walked straight past her and into / the

David   Who was it?

Stella   Like that thing with dogs and their reflex, when they have an automatic, a reflex to /

David   Sorry, but who let you in?

Beat.

Because if you are not an employee then you cannot /

Stella   I used to work for you /

David   If you are not a current employee you cannot actually . . .

Stella   It was Chelle /

David   Chelle /

Stella   Michelle Culliford. Because it's automatic. It's not personal of course, you just smile back don't you?

Beat.

How is she?

Beat.

David   Because I am sorry and this might sound /

Stella   I thought she looked, well she looked, looked exactly the same actually but /

David   Because obviously it is always nice to have ex-employees visit the place /

Stella   But Rory must be, what? One? One and a half?

David   Because it is always nice to see a familiar face and so you can come and visit whenever you like, but /

Stella   He must be quite a big boy now /

David   But you just have to let us know that you are coming.

Stella   Must be quite a handful by now. Must be quite a handful for you all.

Beat.

I was right there where you are standing now.

David   Because this might sound unkind, but you cannot just waltz in here without warning us /

Stella   You were standing right /

David   . . . without warning us first.

Stella   You were right there and it was a party and you were standing right / there

David   We can't have that because then it, it becomes, well and this might sound . . . but it becomes a security issue. That is the thing, it becomes a security issue then you see, because you do not actually have security, you do not actually have the security clearance to come in like this now that you do not work here any more.

Beat.

So you see the difficulty I am in now don't you? You see the difficult position you have put / me in now

Stella   You were standing right there and it was a party and Chelle was singing karaoke and my waters broke, just broke, water all over the floor, Chelle's mouth half open, half, her gurning, like she was singing but the volume had been turned down, and all of you all, slowed down and watching her like she was sizzling, like she was that hot and only Clive's face turned to me a whitish now, whitish like a pillow sort of colour, his face like uncooked dough and then the thump, as my body, must have been the sound of me hitting the floor . . . and I woke up . . . I woke up and I opened my eyes and I saw all this light, this strip lighting like we have here and I asked, I was so confused, I asked where all the phones were! Isn't that funny, because I thought I was here in the office, with all of you, with you all, my family and this woman leaned over me, her head all light, like a halo round her head and she told me something and I turned my head, what she said made me turn my head to the right and lying there was a baby with all this jet black hair, and it turned to me and it let out this, face all bunched up like a prune, let out this scream like nothing you have ever heard. And that was when I realised, it wasn't my baby. It couldn't be my baby because if I heard that noise and I heard it like that just wanting and wanting and wanting something I would feel something, it would make me feel something for it . . .

Because the noise of it, of it screaming like that just went (*Indicating*.) straight through me David. It went (*Indicating*.) straight through me.

Pause.

David   I'm going to call . . . if you don't go / security, the security.

Stella   So I waited and smiled and suckled the little runt and left the hospital with the little runty thing and I took it home, took it back to my tiny clean white bedsit and kept it in a box and watched as it grew like a seed in soil on a sill and I changed it and fed it and grew it, grew it like that, from a bean like that until this morning when I lifted it up out of the box to change it and then realised, as I tried to put it back in that its little toes curled up at the end and there wasn't room any more I lifted it out and I took it on the bus, held it close to my heart on the 73 bus and I travelled to your part of town, to where you bought that flat that you and Kirsten share now as a compromise, against the compromise of the house that you wanted to buy and she didn't and I knocked on the door /

David   No /

Stella   I did. I knocked on the door and she opened it. I didn't say much. Didn't need to say much. I just handed him over. Handed her baby, yours and hers, over to her and I walked away. I walked off down the street. Because it never belonged to me. That was the thing. That baby never really belonged to me so I had to give it back.

David   I won't . . . I won't be made to be . . .

Stella (*smiling*)   Like a star.

David   You cannot scare me like /

Stella   Like a star in the firmament, like a great ball of gas in the sky thousands of, really millions of light years away.

David   I won't be blackmailed like this Stella!

Stella That's what it means. That is what Stella means.

The air con suddenly comes back on and the lights return to normal, perhaps they are even a little brighter than they have been before. **Stella** *and* **David** *look up,* **David** *continues to look up through the following.*

Stella I just wanted to let you know I suppose, how grateful I am for what this place taught me, what I learnt in this beautiful, this lovely beautiful sealed office, how grateful I am to you for helping me to understand what I should be, who I should be for you. For you and all of my family here at Scion Communications. All the different things I needed to be for all of you, even if I am not going to, don't think I am going to try to be them any more.

Stella *disappears.*

David *looks round apprehensively. He sits down heavily, winded.*

End.